CHAMPAGNE

ARDENNE

PRODUCTION LECONTE

Éditions ESTEL

BLOIS 41260 LA CHAUSSÉE-ST-VICTOR

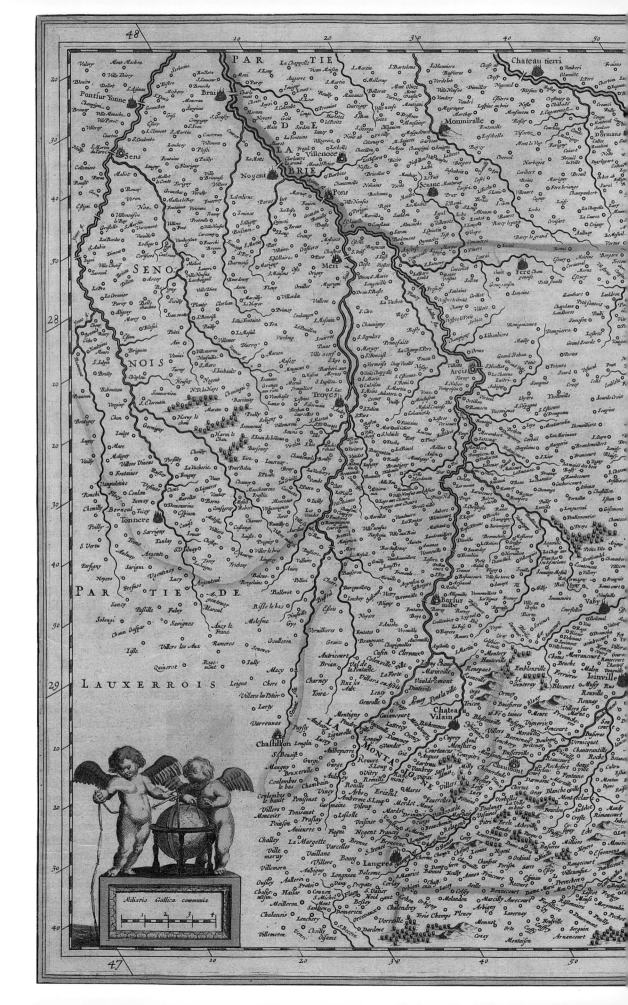

CHAMPAGNE
latine
CAMPANIA,
COMITATVS

Amſterdami
Apud Guiljelmum et Ioannem Blaeu.

PARTIE DV TARTENOIS

Champagne

There is no beautiful region that does not contain areas of very different kinds, just as people have various traits and characteristics, virtues or faults, which make them who they are, resembling other perhaps, but quite unique.

The general term Champagne covers these open and varied regions that are the central plains stretching between the valleys of the Aisne and the Vesle to the north, and that of the Seine in the south, bordered on the east by the first peaks of the Ardennes, those of Argonne, by the Langres plateau to the south-east. It is the north - north-east part of the Paris basin, where limestone, chalk and calcareous clay succeed each other in concentric curves. The plains slope down towards Paris, bordered by steep-sided heavily wooded peaks. The land here is harsh or fertile, light or deep, here retaining abundant water and there free-draining and dry. Champagne really does have a hundred faces. The same diversity will be found in the history of the area, although it takes time to learn how to read the traces of them in its countryside, its villages and towns, designed and built by so many generations before us.

Hundreds of thousands of years ago, along the many rivers in Champagne, first in small family groups then in tribes, our most distant ancestors ventured along the trails they gradually marked out, following the limestone coastline or crossing fords behind herds of wild animals, gathering fruit, seeds and plants, looking for roots and fungi. Their stone tools abound in the silt and Champagne, a land of passage, is one of the richest on the continent in prehistoric tools and weapons. It seems that the region was then deserted for a long period of twenty or thirty thousand years. It is from the tenth millennium before our era that climatic changes altered the countryside, the flora and fauna. The hunter, fisherman, and gatherer of fruit, seeds and plants, would begin around 6000 BC or perhaps 5000 BC, to become a sower of seed for harvesting, raising pigs and cattle, acquiring that peasant farmer outlook which changed hardly at all until our parents' or grandparents' day, and that often we still share, without having lost, even so, the instinct to gather, fish and hunt, which even today draws us to woods, plains and running or still water.

When Caesar arrived in Belgian Gaul, the region had been colonised by several emigrant Celtic peoples, sometimes only a short time before, after a long stay in Germany: the Remi (Marne and Ardennes), the Tongres (Givet point), the Trevires (of the Mouzons area) and the Suessiones (of the Dormans area) - the south of the country was in the hands of the Tricasses (Aube) and the Lingones (Haute-Marne). The Remi, by allying themselves with the Romans, gave Reims a privileged status encouraging the phenomenon of «gallo-romanisation», the mutual assimilation of Gauls and Romans. The major routes from Rome to England and Rome to Germany passed through Langres or Troyes, joined at Châlons then diverged at Reims.

Belated evangelisation began in the big towns in the 3rd century. Sixtus, the first bishop of Reims, was elected some time after 250. Langres, Troyes and Châlons had to wait until the first half of the 4th century to be evangelised. Later bishops often displayed strong personalities and were to assume considerable responsibilities in the face of the Barbarian threat; as was seen subsequently in 451, at the time of the Hun invasions, before an understanding was reached when the Franks settled in these areas as allies of the Romans.

Relations of the bishop of Reims, St Remi (437-532) with Childéric (464-481), king of the Salian Franks, governor for Rome, then with Clovis, his son king and governor in his turn, are examples of this. Remi recognised them as kings of the Franks and representatives of Rome but permitted himself to define with authority their duties as kings, as the letter written to the young Clovis on his accession shows, who was then still a pagan. The bishops of Champagne were to play a major and often fortunate role with the Merovingian kings, or their palace mayors, then with the Carolingians, for four centuries of chaotic and barbaric history, still rumbling with the destructive upheavals of the immense empire, when the invasions resumed in the 9th century and Saracens surged out of the East and the Vikings from Scandinavia.

Charlemagne's peace did not survive the break-up of the empire. At the end of the 9th century, his descendants reigned over seven independent kingdoms, France, Navarre, Lorraine, Burgundy, Provence, Germany and Italy. Little by little, the families governing the great fiefs, marquises, counts and dukes, in a kingdom increasingly part of the Carolingian heritage in name only, ensured the independence of their own domain. The counts of Paris replaced the last Carolingians in a sort of alternation until the election, by the great lords in 987, of Count Robert I's grandson, Hugues-Capet, ancestor of all the kings of France.

In the same period the ambition of Herbert de Vermandois, a direct descendant of Charlemagne, became evident. His eldest daughter married Thibaud le Tricheur [the Cheat], count of Tours, Blois and Chartres. He managed to get his eldest son, Hugues, appointed archbishop of Reims, when he was five years old, thus providing himself with immense revenues; another son, Herbert, became count of the Palace of the Carolingian Lothar; another, Robert, was count of Meaux and of Troyes. In 1022, the latter's grandson, Etienne, left his counties of Troyes and Meaux to his cousin Eudes II le Champenois, grandson and heir of Thibaud le Tricheur. His son was Thibaud I of

Ardenne

Champagne, who was to sire by Gersent du Mans, Etienne-Henri and by Adele de Bar-sur-Aube, his second wife, Hugues.

Etienne-Henri, count of Blois and Meaux, commanded the crusade and was killed at Ramleh in 1102. Hugues, his half-brother, count of Champagne, became a Templar, disinheriting his son in favour of Thibaud II, eldest son of Etienne-Henri. The second son of Etienne-Henri became king of England. [Stephen]

Thibaud II then owned Blois, Meaux and Champagne. His eldest son, Henri, called the Generous or the Liberal, chose the county of Champagne, he married Marie de France, daughter of Louis VII and Eleanor of Aquitaine, left Blois to his brother Thibaud; his second brother, Guillaume of the white hands, was archbishop of Reims; his sister Adèle married Louis VII, divorced from Eleanor. She was to become the mother of Philip-Augustus, grandfather of Louis IX (St. Louis).

Henri the Liberal had two sons. The elder, Henri II, married Isabelle, queen of Jerusalem. The second, Thibaut III, count of Champagne, married Blanche of Navarre. Their son, Thibaut IV, the Troubadour, the Posthumous, count of Champagne and Brie, became, in addition, king of Navarre, his stepfather having had no children. He sold the counties of Blois, Chartres, Sancerre and Châteaudun to king Louis IX; Marguerite of Bourbon gave him two sons, Thibaut V, son-in-law to Louis IX, died in 1270, on his return from the eighth crusade, without an heir; his brother Henri succeeded him, married Blanche of Artois and died in 1274. Their only child, Jeanne, countess of Champagne and queen of Navarre married king Philip the Fair; their three sons, kings of France and counts of Champagne, reigned in succession, the last direct Capetians; Louis X the Quarrelsome, Philip V the Long, Charles IV the Fair, all met a tragic fate.

The history of Champagne then became inextricably linked to that of France, whose kings had already succeeded in removing Reims, Châlons and Langres from the authority of the counts, entrusting them to the seigniorial bishops, great vassals of the king.

This genealogy and two centuries of independence created a picture of prestigious alliances and the house of Champagne always figured among the leading Houses of the west, distinguishing itself in the crusades with their vassals; in literature, in the reigns of Henri the Liberal, whose wife protected Chrétien de Troyes, and of Thibaud IV, the leading poet and musician of his day; but also in economic matters, through the very early freedoms granted to the bourgeois of loyal towns and the institution of the famous fairs of Champagne.

Of sixteen European fairs in the late 12th and 13th centuries, six were held in the county of Champagne which at that time encompassed the eastern edge of Brie, one at Lagny, two in Provins, two in Troyes and one at Bar-sur-Aube, spread over the four seasons and covering the entire year since each lasted about two months; eight days of franchise sales, ten days selling cloth, leathers and goods by weight and the last fifteen days were devoted to settling accounts. Since Sundays and public holidays, of which there were many in those days, were not included, the thirty three days for which the fair was open extended over a two month period. Security for the merchants at the fair and on the roads, and of debts, was provided by a special police corps, notaries, procurators, lieutenants, a hundred and twenty mounted sergeants and twenty on foot. The nations attending the fairs formed leagues, under the authority of an elected captain. The Italians, Lombards and Tuscans had the monopoly of banking transactions. They lived in residence, frequenting the court and the town, sensitive to the arts, knowledge, and were imbued with the spirit of a principality as strong as that of an Italian state, where lords and merchants of all nationalities mixed and where the early seeds of humanism and the Renaissance were to develop into the «quattrocento», in Italy and be returned to us a hundred years later. At the end of the 13th century, the captain of the Italians of Champagne was one Albert de Médicis! With the loss of independence, the fairs survived only about twenty years. The king and the merchants of Paris already had the French instinct for centralisation. Champagne then developed its traditional industries, cloth, hosiery, paper, metallurgy and knife making and traded in its agricultural produce, cereals and wine.

On travelling through the region it will be seen that war rarely left a province very exposed on the eastern and northern frontiers in peace, It was a battlefield during the Hundred Years War, where the Armagnacs and Anglo-Burgundians confronted each other: a battle field of the wars between François I and Charles Quint, continued under Henri II, resumed in the name of the Catholic and Reformed religions, after the disastrous day of Wassy in Champagne, when Henri de Guise had the members of the reformed church massacred, because they sang their psalms too loudly, until the coronation of Henri IV. Then came the Thirty Years War, the Fronde, the wars of Louis XIV, the French campaign at the end of the Empire, the war of 1870 and the two world wars. Champagne suffered harshly, battered by combat, pillaged by armies, but always rose again to draw on the best of itself as it has always done from the beginning of Time.

REIMS. The Remi, a long-haired Celtic clan of Gaul, had conquered an area roughly corresponding to the départements of Marne and Ardennes. They established their stronghold, the fortified town of Durocortorum, on a plain, in the middle of a shallow basin on the Vesle. Little use seems to have been made of this defensive post. It is true that with the sudden arrival of Caesar on the frontier of the Belgica region of Gaul, where he had heard that the clans were mobilising, the Remi, who did not join this coalition, sent him two of their chiefs as ambassadors, Iccium and Antebrogium, to conclude an alliance, declaring their disagreement with the other Belgians elsewhere allied with the Germanic tribes from the other side of the Rhine, (Caesar, The Gallic Wars I-2). This alliance, hastily agreed by Caesar, never broke down, earning the Remi the status of friends of the Roman People, and Durocortorum that of capital of Belgica. The town was to remain one of the pillars of Roman civilisation until the collapse of the Western Empire in 476, and well beyond; for the Church and Clovis had each absorbed the Roman legacy, and the combined effect was to give Roman civilisation the force of a Renaissance whose influence is felt even today.

The first Gallo-Roman buildings were constructed outside the citadel during the first century BC. Around the middle of the next century, the fortified town disappeared, the ditches were filled in and Durocortorum developed in the Roman style, but very gradually. Districts were defined by two main intersecting streets, North-South and East-West with a forum where they crossed, today the site of la Place Royale. Temples and baths, a theatre and amphitheatre were completed only towards the end of the Antonin period, in the last quarter of the second century AD. The Remi capital reached its apogee and had almost 20,000 inhabitants. This garrison town was also a commercial centre, at the cross-roads of the Roman roads to Trèves, Boulogne and Lyons with large numbers of craftsmen and workshops established in the outlying districts including potters, glass-makers and makers of bone objects. Four ceremonial gateways marked the entrances to the walled town at each point of the compass. Aqueducts supplied running water. The PAX ROMANA, until the first quarter of the 3rd century, made life without fortifications possible. Nothing visible now remains of this town except the Mars gate and the gateway crypt, a vaulted underground gallery, the upper quarter of which is lit and ventilated by small windows level with the paving of the forum. You can visit the same type of underground gallery beneath the ancient forum in Arles.

In 235, with the first attempted Barbarian invasions, the town was fortified, nonetheless, in 275, the Franks and Alemanni devastated the country and destroyed the walled town in the anarchy of the end of the Roman Empire. Durocortorum then reconstructed an enclosing wall with the stones from its ruined buildings and took the name of the City of the Remi. Diocletian, Emperor from 284 to 305, restored order and power. The town became capital of the Second Belgica, made up of twelve towns.

The Christianisation of the town began towards the second half of the 3rd century. Saint Sixtus, the first bishop, was elected in about 250. The first basilica was constructed during the 4th century, dedicated to the Apostles. In the 5th century, the site of the cathedral was moved west, to another church, by bishop Saint Nicaise, later beheaded by the Barbarians on the square in front of his cathedral.

Of the new cathedral, dedicated to Mary, the Saviour's mother, during restoration after the Great War, the altar and baptistery were discovered, where Clovis, son of Childeric and grandson of Merovech, received, having been converted by his wife, the Catholic Burgundian princess Clothilde, the baptism he asked for at the hands of Saint Remy, the fifteenth bishop, and a great many other bishops who came from provinces not controlled by the Aryan Visigoths, together with 3,000 of his warriors.

A Carolingian cathedral, begun in 817 and completed in 862 by the bishops Ebbon and Hincmar, replaced the ancient basilica where Louis the Pious, Charlemagne's son, had just received, in 816, the unction and crown from Pope Stephen IV, a reminder of Clovis' baptism and

foreshadowing the establishment of the coronation ceremonies of the kings of France. Three kings were crowned at the abbey church of Saint Remy and thirty in the cathedral, from Louis VIII to Charles X, with only two exceptions - Henry IV, who was crowned at Chartres; and Louis XVIII who dispensed with the holy unction. The value of this blessing was particularly marked through the coronation, on 17 July 1427, of Charles VII, who, having been persuaded by Joan of Arc to demonstrate his legitimacy in way that could never be disputed, was conducted by her to the holy city of Reims.

The brilliance of this episcopal See shone all over Europe from the 9th to the mid 12th century, because of the quality of its teaching dispensed by masters at the canonical school reorganised by Hincmar, archbishop in 845 and an intimate of Charles the Bald. In 972, the monk Gerbert d'Aurillac, studied logic and became director of studies, reorganising them. The king frequently stayed at Reims and the royal school trained the élite of the day. Fulbert, future bishop of Chartres, was a student at Reims with Robert de France, who became king in 996. Gerbert left Chartres to become Pope Sylvester II. In the 11th century the school was one of the homes of humanism and theology in Europe, inspired by Hermann and by Bruno of Cologne, who in 1084 founded la Grande Chartreuse. At the beginning of the 12th century, Alberic, master theologian of the Reims school, refuted the Theory of the Trinity propounded by the celebrated Abelard who had retired to Le Paraclet near Nogent-sur-Seine. Then came the decline. The school prepared students for the new universities, such as Paris. An Ardennes native, Robert de Sorbon, a villein's son and a pupil at the Reims school, left to study in Paris and became Canon of Notre-Dame, an intimate of Saint Louis, and joint founder with the king, of the Sorbonne, which still bears his name.

The cathedral, dedicated to the Virgin and the Saviour, was enlarged in the 10th century and in the 12th embellished with a main façade and a choir imitating that of Saint-Denis. On the 6 May 1210, it burnt down and archbishop Aubri de Humbert decided to construct the building which, despite the immense disaster of the Great War, was to remain the ideal cathedral, dedicated to Notre-Dame [Our Lady].

On 6 May 1211 he laid the first stone and for the first twenty years, work continued with great and constant activity until violent riots between 1233 and 1235 brought the population of Reims into conflict with their lord archbishop. The dispute was not settled to the advantage of the landed gentry, the masons and sculptors returned and the carters resumed work, so well that on 8 September 1241 the chapter celebrated the office in the chancel that already extended the transept and the first bays of the nave. By the end of the 13th century, the whole of the structure was complete so that in 1299 Philip the Fair released the rights to the lead supplied for the roof covering.

Page 9: north transept, left portal: the Last Judgement - Above: the West rose window, consecrated to the Assumption (late 13th century) - Opposite: the façade from the interior, a unique example of interior decoration, seen here from bottom to top, Melchisedech, Abraham, some of the prophets, the announcement of the births of the Virgin Mary, Christ and John the Baptist, scenes from the lives of Christ and John the Baptist, and at the very top, the coronation of a king. - Page 11: the nave. Until the 18th century, a rood screen and chancel wall enclosed the sanctuary proper.

In the 14th century, the gallery of kings was installed. The towers rose slowly, war was never ending, there was famine and epidemics, armies ravaged the herds, fields and vineyards, money was short. In 1481 the timber frame was engulfed by fire and spires had to be finally abandoned. The maze level with the third and fourth bays from the portal, through which the pilgrims could walk while praying, was demolished in 1778. was a square, with an additional polygon at each corner, like a fortress with four towers. In each of them was carved the face of a master craftsman together with an inscription. On the south-east, Jean d'Orbais, who drew up the plans «which began the coif of the church» (the apse with radiating chapels); on the north-east, Jean le Loup «who was master of the church for sixteen years and began the portals»; on the north-west, Gaucher de Reims, master for eight years «who worked on it to the archivolts and portals»; on the south-east, Bernard de Soissons, master for thirty-five years, «who made five vaults and worked on it as far as the O.» (façade). In the centre of the square the archbishop who initiated the work, Aubri de Humbert, was represented.

Mismanaged by the Canons of the 18th century, who had no hesitation in replacing the 13th century stained glass windows with plain glass panes, breaking up the rood-screen and the enclosing chancel wall, Notre-Dame de Reims, almost entirely spared by the «sans-culottes» of the Revolution, was virtually destroyed by systematic bombardment between 1914 and 1918 - 287 shells were counted. Its reconstruction was supervised by the architect Henri Deneux, until 1938, and has continued without pause in the wake of this experience.

The unity of cathedral, its balance, strength and impact were given to it by the first architect, Jean d'Orbais, designer of the plans and model of the work; the high double vaulted bays, bearing a six-petalled rose, can

considered symbolic of the man who built the apse with its radiating chapels.

Jean le Loup developed the initial project with inspiration, giving the cathedral its volume and size. It was he who constructed the buttress topped with pinnacles, where angels with open wings keep watch between heaven and earth; it was he too, who erected the double flying buttresses supporting, between the windows, the openwork wall.

We now know that the façade was erected only in the second half of the century, and thus by the last two architects, Gaucher de Reims and Bernard de Soissons who gave it a strong relief, with the depth of the three portals, whose instructional statuary precedes entrance to the house of God, just as the spoken liturgy precedes the celebration of the Eucharist. Light from the windows replaces the traditional stone tympa accentuating the elevation of the barrel vaulting which are extended by the immense gables up to the level of the great rose window and the windows.

Art historians have identified four quite distinct studios in the sculpture work of the portals, pinnacles and galleries. The first, early 13th centu inspired by Chartres, produced prophets with inspired faces marked by their direct relationship with God. They stand to the right-hand side

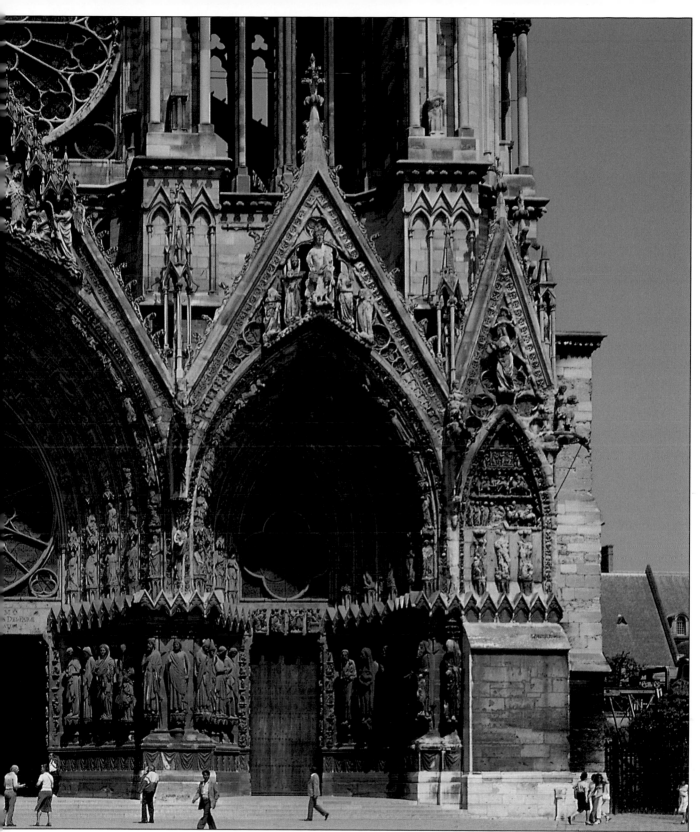

south portal of the west front, from outside to in, they are Aaron, Abraham, Moses, Isaiah, John the Baptist and Simeon. Their pose is ⸻erent and grave. The work of the second studio displays, in a way surprising in the first half of the 13th century, the influence of Hellenic and ⸻man art, that had generally disappeared in the West since the 5th century and was not to reappear until the Italian Renaissance in the 15th ⸻tury. These sculptors owed their style to the tradition of the gold and silversmiths of the Meuse, from which they retained a certain heaviness ⸻he movement of the body, and to their contact with the remnants of Roman statuary, still very numerous in Reims, and indeed with the Greek ⸻rks discovered at the time of the crusades, in Greece and Asia Minor. In the Virgin of the Visitation, on the central portal, there is a perfection ⸻ine worthy of antiquity, with a quality of inner stillness that contrasts with the expression of the figures of the later studios by sculptors from ⸻iens, characters from the Annunciation and the Presentation, on the same central portal. Last come the latest works, dating from the ⸻inning of the second half of the 13th century, made by itinerant sculptors from Champagne or Paris, elegantly draped, spiritual faces with ⸻ond eyes, portraits of unconventional individual beauty, that the smiling angels of Reims have made famous.

⸻ portals and façade are consecrated to the Redemption, stressing the role of Our Lady, to whom the sanctuary is dedicated.

...used statues stand in the shelter of the portals of the north transept, certainly intended ... the first design of the main façade then abandoned for those of new studios. On the ...ht, a small full arched door, beneath the protection of a Virgin and Child (late 12th ...tury), on the left, a portal whose tympan shows the Last Judgement (page 9) and Christ ...the attitude called «Beau Dieu», alas decapitated during the Great War, stands on the ...r, attended by six apostles, the faces are beautiful although their bodies are fairly ...dely carved, except for those of Peter and Paul, to the left and right of Christ.
...e central door has saints of the diocese of Reims grouped around the pope Saint ...ixtus, whose relics were honoured in the cathedral; Nicaise and Remy, the best loved, ...pear both on the tympanum and at the sides. Saint Nicaise holds his decapitated head in ...hands. It was through these three doors, which open on to the cloisters, that the ...ons entered the chancel.

The Roman metropolis of Belgica Secunda, of which the Mars gate is still a reminder, became, with the alliance between Saint Remy and Clov of the Catholic church and the French kingdom, the archiepiscopal and royal metropolis of a vast region. The importance of the Archbishop Reims asserted itself under the Merovingians and then under the Carolingians. He was a great lord from the birth of the French kingdom, a pe of the realm, and was to be a duke from 1319. When he was not a saint - and there were some in the long line of archbishops - he forgot that was the servant of the poor and often became a demanding and harsh master. Reims in the 10th, 11th and 12th centuries was an ecclesiastic principality. Five episcopal fortresses guarded the city, shared between the bishop and his chapter. The southern faubourgs belonged to t Benedictine abbots of Saint Remy and Saint Nicaise; their abbeys were fortified within their own defensive walls.

However, in the Episcopal and royal town, independent of the counts of Champagne, the inhabitants were not all clergy or the archbishop people or canons, the Remis were weavers, wool workers, wine growers, artisans of all trades and merchants. Some families became rich ai formed a kind of patriarchy, part of which, supported by craftsmen, was very gradually to seek to shake off the yoke of the archbishop or obtain concessions from him and a share in the running of their town. It took centuries to obtain from the king the weakening, to both the advantage and his, of a lord so powerful that he dictated their material and spiritual lives and that the king himself had made powerful to redu the power of the counts of Champagne during their two centuries of independence. It took a long time to undo what had been done and reintegrate into the province of Champagne the three cathedral towns of Reims, Châlons and Langres, once taken from the count.

The construction between 1756 and 1760 of la Place Royale by Legendre, royal engineer of bridges and roads, in the Roman heart of t episcopal city, marks, just before the end of the monarchy, the belated equilibrium between central power, the power of the people of Reim symbolised by the Hôtel-de-Ville [Town Hall] constructed between 1627 and 1676, and that of the archbishop, manifest in the modification a

construction of the archbishop's palace, the old ...thic building, known as Tau, because of its T ...aped layout. This was, from 1671 to 1693, the ...rk of archbishop Charles Maurice Le Tellier and ...hitects Robert de Cotte and Pierre Jeunehomme, a ...ive of Reims. Fortunately they retained the 13th ...ntury double two-storey chapel, on the south side ...the cathedral apse with its radiating chapels. The ...ace of Tau, today a museum, presents remnants of ...e original cathedral statuary, tapestries and ...asures, with some wonderful and rare pieces in ...ch of these categories.

...hatever the cost, a symbol of Reims and its ...rtyrdom between 1914 and 1918, the cathedral ...d to be rebuilt. But it was not possible to raise ...m the ruins most of the old residential buildings, ...vate mansions, modest houses, churches and ...nvents of a town that had had so many. According ...a 17th century panoramic map, as a «virtual» ...veller arriving from the west, you see the town ...etched out before you on the far side of the Vesle, ...oking into its ramparts, from the Mars gate in the ...rth to the Saint-Remi gate in the south, and in ...dition to the bell towers, some fifteen parish or

Above: The palace of Tau, eastern façade, with the chapel to the right.
Left: rue de l'Arbalète, the La Salle mansion (16th century).
Below: Place du Forum, the Le Vergeur mansion (16th century) combined several houses for Nicolas le Vergeur, a financier.
Opposite page, top: The Mars gate, a Roman monument, second half of the 2nd century, whose central arch bears a calendar of the work of the four seasons. Notice the reaper, or vallum, with toothed cutting bar 1.30 m wide and the side-fitted device for making the sheaves.
Opposite page, bottom: Place Royale

...nvent churches, as well as the cathedral, and the ...urches of Saint-Remi and Saint-Nicaise. Some are ...rrounded by large estates - Saint-Denis, the ...ominicans, the Cordeliers, various successive ...forms over the centuries and recourse for the ...tizens of Reims against the authority of the ...chbishops. Some of these prelates, moreover, in ...e 16th and 17th centuries, manifest a willingness to ...form, contemporary with the Lutheran reforms, a ...llingness to battle in other ways and from within, ...ainst the laxity of the Church. Archbishop Charles ...Lorraine, 1538 to 1574, made considerable efforts ...this direction, with the effective support of a ...oportion of the inhabitants of Reims.

...he La Salle family was very probably one of these, ...family of prominent citizens, owner of a fine ...ivate Renaissance mansion where Jean Baptiste de ...Salle was brought up. The young man embarked ...an ecclesiastical career and renounced all his ...orldly goods in order to found, in 1685, the Institut ...s Frères des Ecoles Chrétiennes, for the education ...the children of poor families. His order has been ...major educator in France to this day.

...om the earliest beginnings of the kingdom of ...ance, life in Reims has been sung in two registers - ...ergy chanting and celebrating in so many churches, ...ten combining choirs, musical instruments and the ...und of organs, accompanied by bells, fanfares and

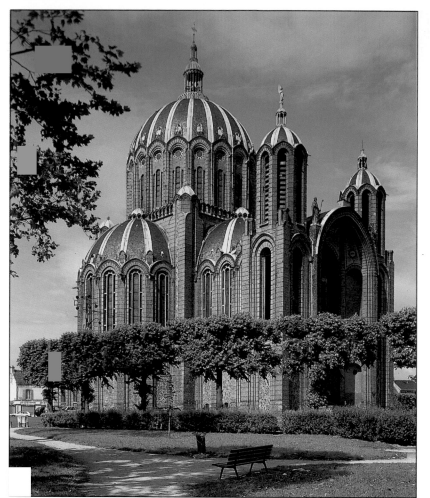

on glorious coronation days, by acclamations of «Joyeus
entrée» [the French equivalent of Vivat Rex or Regina
while the cortège made its way in procession from Sain
Remi to Notre-Dame. The second register is that of th
weavers - both men and women - songs about cloth-makin
accompanied by the clattering of the looms on which the
made, thread by thread, the earlier fortunes of Reim
inhabitants. There are now fewer chants and clergy. Sinc
the Second World War, the mechanised looms, whic
replaced the old machines, have stopped; other industrie
occupy the citizens and Fame, that goddess of deligh
prefers to celebrate the art of making and sellin
Champagne. The vine
come down to the gate
of the town, cella
beneath the old tow
are temples to th
creation of the mos
spiritual and joyful c
beverages ever devise
by Nature and Ma

Above: the basilica of Ste-Clothilde, built by the local architect Alphonse Gosset (1898-1905), dedicated to the Queen of the Franks, wife of Clovis, who spent the last fourteen years of her life at the abbey of St-Martin de Tours, humble and withdrawn from the world, and died in 548, 37 years after Clovis. Top right: Chapelle de la Paix [Chapel of Peace] architect Clauzier, murals, stained glass windows, wrought-iron work by Foujita. Below: Place d'Erlon, the Subé fountain (1906), architect Narjoux; sculptors Gaso, Auban, Bazalis and Wary. Right: Place d'Erlon, the fountain.
Opposite page : The West front of St-Remi.

When Saint Remy died in 533, at a great age, after fifty three years as bishop, his body was immediately placed in the oratory dedicated to Sai Christopher, of one of the oldest cemeteries in Reims, to the south of the town. Very quickly the large numbers of pilgrims made the constructio of a large church necessary, enlarged and rebuilt several times and placed under the authority of the Benedictines by Archbishop Tilpin at t end of the 8th century, a strong personality without doubt since he was to be the model for the valiant Archbishop Turpin who died with Rolan after running through «with Almace, his sword of burnished steel» so many Saracens. Hincmar, the archbishop of Reims who completed tl Carolingian cathedral in 852, also had the Saint Remi basilica restored, in haste, undoubtedly, for fifty years later it was once again in very po condition. In 1005 the abbot Airard began a new abbey church, of which Thierry, his successor, retained only that part of the foundations neede for his own, more modest, project. By about 1039, work was underway; when the wall and galleries were finished Hincmar's old abbey churc could be completely demolished, and the monks' choir stalls temporarily covered, who could then sing the holy office without being exposed the elements. Abbot Thierry died in 1045, Hérimar, his provost, succeeded him and had the works completed, covering the structure with timber frame for which the monks selected the wood from the forest of the abbey of Orbais. The Alsatian pope, Leon IX, Brunon d'Eguishein Dabo, consecrated the church in October 1049. Such, in essence, is the direct and valuable evidence of one of the monks of Saint Rem Anselme, a contemporary witness.

The chancel wall and tomb of Saint Remy, restored from parts of the 16th century tomb, destroyed in 1793. Page 20, the nave and chancel.

f the abbey basilica, whose construction was seen by Anselme with his own eyes, remains us today the eleven Romanesque bays of the nave and transept. The nave was preceded by two-storey fore-nave, as evidenced by the turret staircase on the right. The transept crossing as the same height as the nave, but the arms were lower and narrower. Their barrel-vaulted est aisles were narrow than the east which opened into east-facing chapels. The pillars, anks of fourteen alternating large and small columns stood on a heptagon, then a round linth and was decorated with stucco capitals, a process inherited from the Carolingians, more ften kept in the Germanic Holy Roman Empire with which Reims maintained links; thus the lsatian pope, Leon IX, who came to consecrate the new abbey church, was a close relative f the emperor Henry III. Saint Remy's tomb was in the chancel, then a simple apse. On the utside, walls bearing the weight of a timber frame and not vaults, was supported by applied uttresses in the form of columns, still visible in several places.

n the 1160s, Pierre de Celle, abbot of Saint-Remi, had the fore-nave replaced by two gothic ays in the Romanesque nave extension, adding, between the gallery and the upper windows, triforium - a small gallery of double-bays. He had the Romanesque apse replaced by a iple-bay chancel with double aisle - first the ambulatory around the chancel provided room or pilgrims to circulate around the tomb of Saint Remy and on coronation days the rocession of clergy coming to fetch the Holy Oil [used only for the blessing of the monarch his coronation] kept near the saint's shrine. Four radiating circular chapels and a central hapel with four bays and an apse doubled the ambulatory. The same triforium runs between

he gallery and the upper windows. The new chancel was finished in the 1180s.
ollowing which work on vaulting the transept was undertaken by raising in front
f the Romanesque pillars columns bearing smaller columns carved with the grain
f the stone, pointed arches strengthening the wall, above the tribune openings.
he nave was then refurbished and vaulted using the same technique. On the
utside, buttresses and flying buttresses of the greatest simplicity provided support
t the upper gallery level and the top of the gutter wall. The façade, whilst fairly
nodest for a building of such generous interior size, nonetheless has something of
Roman grandeur with superimposed openings of portals and windows framed by
luted classical pilasters and columns, borrowed from the buildings of the imperial
ity, and, on two high columns on either side of the bay surmounting the central
ortal, the statues of Saint Peter and Saint Remy, on their own, without the usual
oly throng of the portals of the period. The first two levels, (the remainder,
xcept the right bell tower, were redesigned in the 19th century) - evoke for a
noment the façade of a basilica or a Roman amphitheatre. Who could be
stonished at such influences, so much do all the ancient travellers' tales describe
he Gallo-Roman ruins they discovered before coming to the ramparts of the town.
he 12th century stained glass windows form an admirable set of distinguished
eople, kings, prophets, bishops and patron saints, to be returned to again by the artists of the 13th
entury.

n the north aisle of the nave, a fragment of 14th century paving, whose slabs are engraved and the lines
illed with lead, represents scenes from the Old Testament, in a style related to that of the miniatures
nd wood engravings of the same period. These slabs come from the abbey church of Saint Nicaise
which was just to the east of Saint Remi. The second large Benedictine abbey in Reims, the church
f Saint Nicaise, a prodigious Gothic success virtually contemporary with the cathedral, was sold by
he revolution and dismantled stone by stone, for use as building material. The tomb stone of
Hugues Libergier, its architect, was moved into the cathedral. The church also held a
econd century white marble sarcophagus, portraying a lion hunt, which is said to have
een used as the tomb of consul Jovin, who died in 370, founder of a basilica to St.
Agricola, which preceded the first St. Nicaise church. This sarcophagus is now in the
aint-Remi museum, together with numerous historic items and works of art.

*Above: the entombment (1531). Below: south side, flamboyant façade of the transept
early 16th century). Opposite page: the nave and its crown of light (reconstruction).*

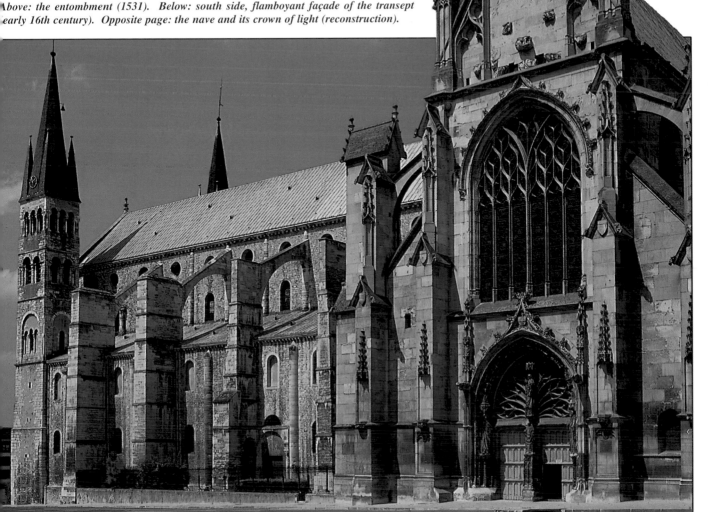

CHAMPAGNE

The vineyards of champagne cover the chalk hillsides which rise from the valleys, hillsides often crowned with coppiced woodland, the domain, in years gone by, of wood-cutters and charcoal burners. It was from here too that supplies of stakes and poles for the vines were obtained, for before wire was used for staking, the shoots of each vine stock were tied in to its own stake. The trees in this fairly poor soil develop in a curious way, sometimes, like the «faux de Verzy» (from the Latin fagus, a beech tree) whose branches twist horizontally instead of growing upwards in clusters as this species usually does. They seem, strangely, to want to imitate the vine plants. The villages are in the valleys, surrounded by gardens and fields of grain. This vineyard currently extends over almost 30,700 hectares, of which approximately 22,770 are in the Marne, 5,870 in the Aube, a little over 2,000 in the Aisne, and less than 20 in each of the départements of Seine-et-Marne and Haute-Marne.

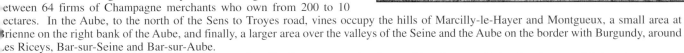

7% of the land holdings are shared by 15,500 wine-growers and the rest between 64 firms of Champagne merchants who own from 200 to 10 hectares. In the Aube, to the north of the Sens to Troyes road, vines occupy the hills of Marcilly-le-Hayer and Montgueux, a small area at Brienne on the right bank of the Aube, and finally, a larger area over the valleys of the Seine and the Aube on the border with Burgundy, around Les Riceys, Bar-sur-Seine and Bar-sur-Aube.

The wild vine, vitis vinifera, probably grew naturally, climbing amongst the elms and hornbeams offering its clusters of fruit to hunters and gatherers whose families, in prehistoric times, roamed the peaks and wooded slopes of Champagne, but no-one knows whether or not they made a fermented drink from it. The Celts, however, who came from the East to colonise Gaul, were familiar with fermentation into alcohol, brewing beer and keeping it in barrels. They were familiar with wine because they had travelled through Greece and Italy as warriors and traders. It seems, however, that it was not until Latin colonisation that they planted vines. This was such a rapid success that the emperor Domitian, ordered them to be rooted up to protect Italian wines from serious competition barely a century after Caesar's conquest.

The next emperors probably permitted Gaulish vine cultivation, and under Marcus Aurelius, the Mediterranean amphora was completely replaced by the Celtic barrel. Finally, the vine resisted the Barbarian invasions and the archbishop of Reims, Saint Remy, dying at the age of 96 on 13 January 533, could in his will, bequeath six vines, one planted by his own hands, at Vendresse in the Ardennes - the planted area was then larger than it is today.

The vine, in all civilisations where its cultivation was possible, is closely enmeshed with the very fabric of that society, in symbols, decoration, tradition, literature and religion. It had an important place in Judaism, and later in Christianity. The texts of the Old Testament contain a wealth

Page 24. Marne Valley, the vineyard rising from the village to the wooded hilltop.
Above: «faux de Verzy» - Below: «Montagne de Reims» [the Mountain of Reims], grape harvesting at Verzenay.

of passages referring to the vine and wine, and those of the New Testament more still with the vine, wine presses and wine as recurring symbols and Christ even associated wine, like bread, with the mystery of the sacrament itself It is evident that the Church, taking over from Rome defeated by the Barbarians, had to work to maintain and then develop wine-growing, in the same spirit that led it to preserve and develop the Greco-Roman cultural legacy.

This dual manual and intellectual drive, according to the rule of St. Benedict, had always been led by the Benedictine monasteries; their monks cleared land, erected buildings, planted and applied themselves to copying and transcribing religious and secular texts. The abbey of Hautvillers provides an excellent example of such activities. It was founded in 650 by the twenty-fifth archbishop of Reims, Nivard, and by Saint Berchaire, a monk of the Saint Colomban order, who was shortly to retire into the forest of Der, where the monasteries of Montier-en-Der and Puellemontier were later established The abbey church of Hautvillers was consecrated to Saint Peter and Saint Augustine.

Ebbon, the thirtieth archbishop, first builder of the Carolingian cathedral, former librarian of Aix-la-Chapelle and one of the inspiring forces of the Carolingian Renaissance, made Hautvillers one of its key centres by supporting the scriptorium, in the strict sense a studio of copyist monks, and in fact a Benedictine art and publishing business, nourished by all the knowledge of the day with a theological and spiritual view of the world. Ebbon got the most erudite monks to come there, the best copyists and painters and enhanced the library with numerous ancient works. This Champagne school produced manuscripts of sublime artistry, like the Evangeliary (or gospel book) held by the library at Epernay or the celebrated Psalter of Utrecht.

Alas, the archbishop liked power and intrigue. He conspired against the emperor Louis the Pious and deposed him in order to crown his son Lothar. Louis regained power, Ebbon was tried and in turn deposed in 841, and the artists of Hautvillers were dispersed to other abbeys. Their style is to be found in certain works of Saint Martin of Tours and the palace school of Charles the Bald, and even in some copies made by Anglo-Saxon monasteries in the 10th century.

The intellectual and artistic renown of Hautvillers under the Carolingians equalled that of its wines, both red and white, and, although Ebbon's disgrace led to the dispersal of the great copyists and illuminators, it is probable that the tradition of writing and teaching was maintained here at a less striking level, but faithful to the Benedictine rule, agricultural activity was also continued, ensuring, through the centuries, the self-sufficiency of the vast estate, with a strong emphasis on wine-growing. Devotion to the relics of Saint Helena, mother of Emperor Constantine, increased the monks' prosperity. In 841, their abbot, Teutgise, taking advantage of a journey to Rome, had stolen these relics. He brought back the devotional booty, as was common practice at the time, to his own monastery, developing what we today would call a fashion for religious tourism.

Burned by the Normans in 882, like most of the villages and religious foundations established in the valleys through which their boats travelled, and rebuilt in 940 by abbot Rotmar, Hautvillers then became the feudal overlord and suffered, like all feudal domains, the vicissitudes of the history of Champagne and the kingdom. Pillaged and burned by the English in 1449, the monastery regained its prestige after its reconstruction, when abbot Jean Royer, the last abbot elected, had it restored and improved between 1507 and 1527. The Calvinists in their turn burned the abbey down in 1562, and it was once again restored in 1603. Building and improvements continued throughout the 17th and 18th centuries, bearing the mark of the great prosperity of the abbey estates, to which the very well known Dom Perignon was to make its contribution. Brother Pierre Pérignon, born in 1633 at Sainte-Menehould, entered Hautvillers as a novice when he was very young, and was appointed procurator and cellarer from 1668 to 1715. This post gave him administrative and financial responsibility for all aspects of running the estate. He acquitted himself in exemplary fashion, excelling particularly in the art of planting and cultivating the vines, harvesting and above all, wine-making. Not that he «invented» Champagne wine out of thin air - before his arrival the people of Champagne had been selling a sparkling and distinctive rosé wine, pleasant, light

The church and remains of the cloister at Hautvillers.
The huge statue of Pope Urban II, on the site of the former château of Châtillon.

Dormans chapel, commemorating the two battles ot the Marne (1914 - 1918).

Pinot noir from which the press produces a clear juice.

nd delicately perfumed, but champagne owes much to the procurator of Hautvillers.

Dom Pérignon first directed his efforts at blending wine from different soils, composing a «bouquet» in the same way as composing a perfume. rom the pressing producing a must from the whole, sorted grapes, which had not had time to develop colour, he drew off a juice clear as rock rom Pinot Noir or Pinot Meunier coloured grapes; he then managed to stabilise and ensure good keeping qualities in the bottles of wine he roduced. Temperature controlled cellars maintained at 11/12°C were hollowed out of the chalk hillsides; glass-makers perfected stronger «Champagne» bottles, to prevent breakages which sometimes occurred with two thirds of the bottles. Finally, between 1655 and 1709, the hange from sealing the bottles with a piece of caulked wood, the «broquelet», to the cork stopper was made. It was later, in about 1752, that he practice of racking to remove the sediment became general.

s success was considerable from the end of Louis XIV's reign and under the Regency. It has remained enormously popular. Nor did roduction of red wine from the «montagne» of Reims and the River Marne run dry and was to continue for a long time yet, passing usually hrough local Reims' wine merchants, who sent bottles of champagne wine in crates of 100 and more, and casks of pale and red wines by aterway and cart.

Dom Pérignon passed away on 14 September 1715 at the age of 77, having passed on to his successors his expertise and wine-making secrets, eaving too, the memory of a heart sensitive to the misery of the poor. The lands of the abbey estate were sold as church assets during the evolution, in fairly small plots in order to content a great many wine-growers. The Chandon family of Epernay acquired, amongst other assets, art of the abbey buildings and some of its vineyards.

he history of Hautvillers is a model of the establishment of a Champagne wine-growing estate, renowned since the late Middle-Ages and robably even earlier under the Roman Empire, an example of the blossoming, in the Baroque period when all the arts flourished, of the most piritual, most expressive beverage, the most «cultivated» it could be said, worthy of Marivaux and of Watteaux, of Couperin and Rameau, of Beaumarchais, Mozart ...

he same history can be retraced through the names of the Montagne de Reims, the côte des blancs, the river Marne or the slopes of Aube. Villages and estates have taken shape here and been tilled for almost two thousand years by the wine-rowers who planted, tilled, pruned, cut down, harvested, pressed the grapes and tended the wine in the ellars through good times and bad.

Many of the estates are associated with famous names. A tall statue of Eudes de Lagery, son of a knight of he manor of Châtillon, watches over the vines of Châtillon and Port à Binson. Eudes, canon of the Chapter f Reims and a great Prior of Cluny, preached the first crusade in 1095 at Clermont in Auvergne, later ecoming Pope Urban II. His statue stands on the site of the former château of the illustrious Châtillon amily, now destroyed. Gaucher de Châtillon, grandson of the constable to Philippe-le-Bel, Louis X, Philippe V and Charles IV, defended Reims against the English besieging it, from 4 December 1359 to 11 anuary 1360. Edward III lifted the siege.

Archbishops, emperors, kings and princes, bishops and other lords all had their Champagne wine-press and ineyard. Jean le Bon gave the county of Vertus, south of Epernay, to his daughter Isabelle when she narried Jean Galéas Visconti, the duke of Milan; their daughter Valentine, the countess of Vertus, was narried to the extravagant Louis, duke of Orleans, later assassinated by the people of the duke of Burgundy, ean-sans-Peur [the fearless], in rue Neuve du Temple in Paris, on 23 November 1407. Henry IV, who had ong travelled through the Champagne area, was very fond of Aÿ wine and only too happy to recall he was ts overlord. The village of Dormans was built as the seigniory by queen Joan of Navarre, countess of Champagne and wife of Philippe le Bel, for Jean de Dormans, then was his son's, the bishop of Beauvais. Of their château only two towers remain, flanking the 17th century building constructed, it is believed, for Charles de Broglia, who acquired the Dormans land in 1660. n the grounds, a chapel has been built to commemorate the two battles fought on the Marne during the 914-1918 war.

The church at Aÿ.

The quality of a wine as reputed as champagne must be jealously protected. Wine growers and merchants have obtained, often as the result of conflict of interest, the introduction, in 1905, 1908, 1909 and 1911, of regulations specifying the areas, sizes, variety and methods of cultivatio harvesting and wine-making for champagne. Establishing the boundaries of vineyards producing the grapes used to make wines called «Champagne was, on several occasions, the cause of riots. Owners of recognised vineyards in the Marne district and those of the Aube wine-growing area, who the authorities and the merchants wished to exclude, challenged them, laying waste, setting fires and looting in a rural uprising. It should be pointe out that the merchants could buy the harvests from the Aube at half the Marne prices, and even more cheaply outside Champagne. In 1911, 40,00 troops occupied the Champagne growing area until the harvest. After the 1911 laws were passed, the only Champagne was that made exclusive from classified champagne grapes. Legislation has become increasingly strict since that time. The constraints and restrictions introduced during th 20th century, right up to the present day, has had one purpose only - not just quality, but excellence.

Ripe, healthy grapes are picked by hand, unripe and damaged fruit discarded, then placed, not too tightly packed, into baskets and carried, witho jolting, to vehicles whose suspension is designed to prevent bruising before they arrive at the wine-press, where the first mixing of grape varieties done (usually 75 per cent black grapes to 25 per cent Chardonnay grapes).

The traditional design vertical thrust wine-press, is fitted with a bottom trap so that the juice expressed does not linger in too high a residue and flo rapidly without developing colour or absorbing undesirable elements. It takes four tonnes of grapes to fill one press. The first pressing produc 2000 litres of première cuvée [first vintage from the vats]. The marc [residue] is then «taillé» or turned and then put back into the press, and w give, on the first and second turning, another 550 litres at most, which will make wines of the first and second «taille». The last «taille» or turnin gives a must unsuitable for wine-making which will be distilled.

The contents of the vats are then put to ferment in barrels or vats and decanted for the first time in third week. A second decanting takes place after clarification by cooling, in the not so distant p advantage was taken of the first frosts. In spring, the wines of different years, varieties and vintages blended. Very good years are confined to vats of the most recent harvest to produce a vint. champagne, while in general, blending is done with vats of the latest vintage combined with the vinta of other years whose qualities complete and balance the wine to suit the taste of the wine-maker and customers. The blended wine is then bottled, natural champagne fermenting agents are added to caus second fermentation or «prise de mousse» [letting the «sparkle» develop] lasting several months causing the pressure to rise to 6 bars. It is then that the bottles are placed in racks at an angle of degrees, head downwards, and turned every day to make the deposit move down towards the neck, f period of between three and five months. The bottles are then stored horizontally in the cool of the h cellars carved out of the chalk.

There remains the task of removing the dregs that have accumulated next to the cork, either by a turn of the hand, or by freezing the top of the neck. The amount removed is made up by add Champagne liqueur. The ageing period before a sweet Champagne is sold is a minimum of one y extra dry champagnes require at least 3 to 5 years.

The character of a wine is the expression of a vineyard, the variety, the weather and seasons of a y and the wine-grower's skill from harvest to bottling, and of the cellars. In a Champagne, these elem are enhanced by blending, and a very complex process of composition, comparable to the wa concerto combines instruments, tones, themes and rhythms. The «blanc de blanc» from a sin Chardonnay rootstock variety, particularly reputed on the Côte des blancs, is thus like a sonata. It is of Champagne as it is of music, it will appeal to the expert's taste, yet will often give just as m pleasure to the amateur.

es 30 and 31: Cellars,
, rooms and racks -
rdonnay.
n Perignon at the
ët et Chandon
ding.

EPERNAY

This name, Sparnacus in Latin and which was known in the 6th century, comes from the Gaulish word «Sparn», a thorn. On seeing the tow surrounded by vine-covered hillsides, topped by small woods, you cannot help but marvel at the work of man in turning thickets into vineyards! Under Clovis, in the late 5th century, Euloge, owner of the estate, sold it to Saint Remi for 5,000 silver pounds to be distributed to the poor. Archbishop Eblé de Roucy resold it to count Eudes de Champagne (11th century) who founded the collegiate church of Saint Martin. Eperna became French with Champagne. Its history is that of the happiness of a prosperous vineyard and the misery of war. It has suffered 25 sieges an been destroyed almost as many times - in the feudal wars; the Hundred Years War ; the war with Charles the Fifth (of Spain) who laid siege to it; th

wars of religion when the walled town was occupied by the Ligueurs; besieged in 1592 by Henry IV, who himself saw the faithful Biron killed at his side by a bullet; the Thirty Years War; Napoleon I's French campaign; 1870 and the Prussian occupation and the martyrdom of 1914-1918, amongst others.

From the 18th century and the growing fame of Champagne, for which Epernay was a trading centre, and competing with Reims, the town acquired great opulence. Mr. Denis, author of a stagecoach travel guide, published in 1770, included this description of Epernay, «There is considerable trade in excellent wines, known by the name of the growing area, Hautvillers, Ay, Avenay, Bernon, Pierry, Avize, Vertus, etc.» and later, «Leaving the boulevards you pass through the Faubourg de la Folie, on rising ground; it is of immense wealth, as can be imagined on seeing the fine newly built mansions; they keep considerable cellars of wine, of the best quality ...»

In the 19th century, the great wine merchants, Girard, Auban-Moët, Moët et Chandon, Charles Perrier, de Venoge, Piper-Heidsieck, Gallice, Mercier, de Castellane, enriched the town with public and private buildings, religious and secular, in the varied styles of a period in which architecture was trying to find itself, with greater or lesser originality and varying success. The visitor of today, a pilgrim to these illustrious wine-cellars, may also find the treasures of the Château-Perrier library and museum of interest.

Page 32: Vines above the Marne and the town of Champagne - Town Hall.
Above: left, the church of Notre-Dame, 1898-1915, inspired by St. Yved of Braine (Aisne). Some fine early 16th century stained glass windows were reused here.
Right, portal of the old St. Martin's church (1540).
Opposite, the Moët et Chandon building, gardens and orangery (1872-1884).

MONTMORT. Jeanne de Hangest built the square keep dwelling enclosed by four round towers dating from 1577 on the base slab of a ruined château. The original base, itself defined by bastions, is accessible via a 15th century spiral connecting ramp, as in the Hurtault tower at Amboise. The black varnished bricks are laid in a pattern reminiscent of the Loire Valley, a legacy, perhaps, of his grandfather, equerry to queen Anne of Brittany.

SÉZANNE, dear to the counts of Champagne, obtained from Thibaut I, two fairs each year, and from Thibaut IV, a commune charter. Its tree-lined walks, over the filled-in moat, mark the outline of the ramparts. After a fire in 1632, it was rebuilt under Louis XIV in brick and rubble stone, rather than the traditional exposed timber framing. The convent of Récollets, constructed outside the walls in the same period, is today used as a hospital. Below, the cloister.

MONDEMENT. The monument, 33 metres high, commemorates the victory of the Marne in 1914. Architect, Paul Bigot - Sculptor, Henri Bouchard.

HALONS-EN-CHAMPAGNE. The walled town owes its name to the Gaulish Catalauni «brave in battle». Founded by the Emperor ocletian in the late 3rd century AD, it removed the south of their territory from the Remi, for an unknown reason. The regional capital, protected a loop in the Marne and by the Mau, one of its branches, (another branch, the Nau, breaks off further east), was then fortified. After the great asions and the defeat of Attila, the walled town remained an important citadel between Troyes and Châlons. Very soon, the bishop was lord of town. In the 10th century he encompassed within its walls the merchants quarter, around St-Alpin church. From the time of the first Capetians, âlons, like Reims, was shielded from the counts of Champagne by being converted into an episcopal county, the principal royal bastion on the tern frontier of the kingdom. The bishop-count was a peer of France. Around the fortified town craft industries and a commercial centre veloped, and the town expanded to be enclosed by the late 12th century, by a third wall which was to define its boundary until the 19th century. ere were a great many tanners along the branches of the Marne, weavers made cloth «le chalons», sold in England and throughout the editerranean, until the economic collapse of the Hundred Years War.

ide the town rose the cathedral and a number of churches, St-Alpin, Notre-Dame-en-Vaux, St-Loup and St-Jean. The finest, certainly, Notre-me-en-Vaux, a canonical church, was completed at the beginning of the 12th century and fell down in the middle of the century. Miracles were d to occur there such that in the general enthusiasm and flood of donations, it was immediately reconstructed, at the same time, probably, as the ister to the left of it, demolished in the 18th century. Archaeological excavations since 1966 have recovered its outstanding statuary. Completed ing the 13th century, Notre-Dame lost favour as a place of pilgrimage to the benefit of Notre-Dame de l'Epine [Our Lady of Thorns], then its ependence, contested by the cathedral chapter. Notre-Dame-en-Vaux is an example of early Gothic architecture. The Nau flows before its main

Notre-Dame-en-Vaux, the apse.

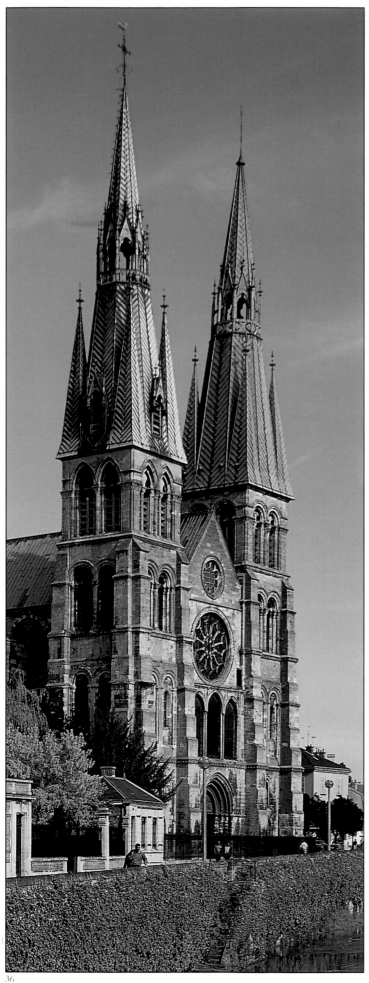

front. Fishermen, once brought the finest fish to the canons, in their boats.

Châlons is built entirely along its three watercourses, making it and its gardens, including the famous Grand-Jard and Petit-Jard, bathed by these waters, a delightfully tranquil town. Most of the old houses were of half-timbered construction, of the local Champagne type, with an upper floor and an attic. Later, their façades were rendered. Many were demolished in the 1970s.

In the days when the bishop was both count and peer of the realm, and carried the royal ring on coronation days, the cathedral must have always had to be spoken of before all else.

The first is mentioned in 560, the next was built in about 1000, and destroyed in the second half of the 12th century. In 1147, Pope Eugene III consecrated a sanctuary here, of which the crypt of Notre-Dame remains. After a further ordeal, it was reconstructed, re-using the still usable consecrated parts. In 1237, with the chancel and transept finished, the offices could be celebrated once more. Saint Louis and his wife, the queen, appeared as donors on one of the stained glass windows. Work then continued, through

Left: Notre-Dame-en-Vaux. Above: château du Marché over the Archers bridge Below: half-timbered houses.

Hôtel-de-Ville [the town hall]

od years and bad, despite numerous setbacks, until the end of the 17th century, in the style of the 13th century, except for the classical façade.

the 15th century, the bourgeoisie had begun to re-appear, and, made wealthy by trade, bought land from the nobility ruined by war. Labourers and vineyard rkers changed masters, but gained nothing - merchants were better accountants than knights.

1588, Châlons, occupied by the «Leaguers», expelled them with the bishop of the day, gaining recognition from Henry III who declared it the «principale ce royale». In the same spirit, the town was to recognise Henry IV as its king, who was to make it the capital of the administrative district of Champagne.

virtue of this status, Châlons gained a number of 18th century historic buildings, such as the Hôtel-de-Ville [town hall] (1772-1776), whose architect, colas Durand, had designed the square; and the Intendance [steward's office] (1759-1771) by the architect Jean Gabriel Legendre. To the last royal steward, uillé d'Orfeuil, goes the credit for having had the Ormesson laid out, the view along the Jard.

Champagne-Ardenne Regional Government building

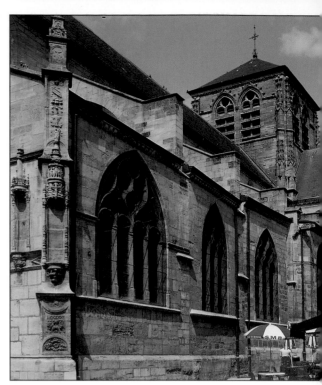

Left, the cathedral, south side - Above, St-Alpin church.

After the revolution and under the regimes that followed, the tow maintained its predominance, despite the power of Reims, its riva Still, in the 18th century, excluding the cathedral, there were twel churches in Châlons, not to mention the twelve abbey monasteries and convents. It is still possible to visit Saint-Lou the oldest parts of which date from the 14th century, Saint-Jea which would have been the town's oldest church had it not bee rebuilt from the 14th to 17th centuries, Saint-Alpin, squeezed in the old merchants' quarter. It was built in the 12th centur vaulting added in the 13th, then provided with a new chancel at t beginning of the 16th century, together with chapels, in as much space permitted, and finally, some fine stained glass windows.

NOTRE-DAME DE L'EPINE.
In the 13th century, t inhabitants of Châlons venerated a miraculous Virgin, two leagu along the Ste-Menehould and Verdun road, found in a thorn bus They prayed to her in a chapel dedicated to John the Bapti belonging to the royal abbey of Saint-Jean in Laon. Constructio of a church was undertaken in 1410, during a disastrous period, f Champagne, of the Hundred Years War, when it was overrun t armed bands of Burgundians and Armagnacs.

A local Châlons mason, Pierre Poutrise, put in charge of the wor used limestone from the Bar district, starting with the nave, t fifth and sixth bays, then the third and fourth and the façade. Wo then moved to the transept and later the chancel. The St. Jea portal for the south transept is reminiscent of the north portal Châlons cathedral; the inscription put up by donors, the mercers Châlons, dates it as 1439. The pilgrimage was such a success, had to be enlarged.

In 1445, gifts from Charles VII permitted two bays to be added, t façade to be rebuilt to suit the earlier architectural design, but in t flamboyant style; and two spires to be erected bearing the Virgin lilies with those of France.

The apse and its chapels added in the first quarter of the 16 century, were completed in 1550, including the altar. The soldie of 1793 broke the statues but an entire population of gargoyles wa saved - devils, monsters and the deadly sins spit out storm wate from between the balusters of the roof. The north tower lost i spire for use as a telegraph pole in 1798; Napoleon III gave on back in 1868.

The West front of Notre-Dame de l'Epine.

VITRY-LE-FRANÇOIS. The capital of Perthois, the alluvial plain between Marne and the forest of Trois-Fontaines, was rebuilt on the banks of the Marne, after Vitry-en-Perthois - on the Saulx, upstream of its confluence with the Marne - was burned to the ground by Charles Quint in 1544. This royal stronghold defended the Paris road.

In 1545, François I had plans for a new site drawn up by Girolamo Marini, an engineer from Bologna, who specialised in fortifications. The previous site, high up, exposed the ramparts to artillery fire, which was becoming increasingly powerful. Flat ground was therefore chosen where the town seemed to hide, the waters of the Marne supplied the moats at the foot of low walls forming triangles with the points of three of them jutting towards the north and three to the south, while a star shaped citadel kept a lookout to the east. The town was laid out on a grid pattern with three straight main roads, from east to west, and in the centre a rectangular parade ground. On this square was built the first wooden church, then, in the 17th century, a church in the classical style, finished in 1755 and dedicated to Notre-Dame [Our Lady].

Of the royal town there remains, after wars and invasions, the layout, a gate moved from the west exit to the north exit, the façade of the collegiate chapel (17th century), and, reconstructed stone by stone, the church of Notre-Dame.

At the end of the 18th century, the traveller taking the stage coach or cabriolet to Châlons at eight o'clock in the morning, arrived at Vitry through the Faubourg de Vaux at about one o'clock in the afternoon, alongside the ramparts on which he would have seen windmills, and passing over water-filled moats then under the Vaux gate. It would have cost him 6 pounds and 88 sous by stage coach, and 4 pounds by cabriolet, without the carriage for his bags. The town at that time had half-timbered houses, with an upper floor and attic. His guide would have told him that the town had a Présidial [Court of Appeal], a Baillage [County Court], an Election [a financial constituency administered by elected representatives], a Constabulary and two Parishes. Notre-Dame, which was also a collegiate church, and St. Germain, a convent of Récollets, Augustines, Minimes and Doctrinal fathers (a teaching order) who ran a College, Dames Régentes (a teaching order of nuns), Grey Sisters, a Hospital ... The local trade included makers of smooth serge, druggets,

muslin, woven goods, millinery, hand-made stockings, cotton and other cloth of any width; braids, half silk and half thread etc. There were also Tanners, markets on Thursdays and Saturdays which did a sizeable trade in oats, taken to Paris via the Marne, a fair on 24 February, which lasted 9 days; another after Easter, and four more, on 22 July, 1 September, on St. Martin's Day and St. Andrew's Day. Passing through the town, there was a fine square quadrangle of about four acres, from the middle of which you could see the four streets that ended in it, of which one was in a direct line from the gate to the Indes bridge under which passed the Marne, on the square itself was a newly built hall, big and spacious - this hall burned down in 1940.

The number of government offices, markets and fairs were the result of François I's desire to secure the resources of the new town, to which he had given his name.

Above: the collegiate church of Notre-Dame - Left: the bridge Gate (18th century) - Below: façade of the college chapel (17th century). These last two buildings have been moved.

VALMY. In 1792, the French troops of Marshal Lückner had attack Belgium and taken Menin and Courtrai before being routed by t Prussians at Baisieux. Relieved of his command, Lückner was sent to guillotine. On 2 September, the Prussians took Verdun. On the 11th, th crossed the heights of Argonne through the Grandpré pass, over-runni some thirty kilometres further north, Dumouriez and Kellermann who w waiting for them at the Islettes pass. On the 20th, 34,000 Prussians, 30,0 Austrians and 6,000 French emigrés were to stand in battle lines to face 52,000 French who had taken up position to their rear, to the west of mill, Kellermann's command post. The day passed in very violent cann fire, according to Goethe, who had accompanied the Duke of Brunswick a volunteer. «The French,» said Goethe, «were immobile, Kellermann h taken a more advantageous position; our men were taken out of the line fire and it was as if nothing was happening, the greatest consternati spread amongst the army. On that morning, we thought of nothing l than running through all those Frenchmen and swallowing them up ...». the 21st, the coalition retreated, struck down by a terrible dysentery wh killed 3000 men. It is said that the German troops had been gorgi themselves in the vines, on which the grapes were not yet ripe. It is a said that Brunswick was bribed to withdraw. This battle with no r engagement, caused 150 mortalities, 260 French wounded, and 160 ene deaths. The mill was burned to the ground; the present mill, of the sa type, was installed in 1947.

SAINTE-MENEHOULD. The rocky outcrop surrounded by the Ais to the west of the forests of Argonne, commands, on the Champagne side, the Islettes pass where the French awaited the Prussians before Valmy. T Roman Gauls had a garrison here. Thibaud III of Champagne obtained it from the count of Rethel who ceded the town to him in 1197. His wido Blanche of Navarrre, mother of Thibaud IV and regent of the County, in 1204 had a fortress built here, awarding its inhabitants a commune char François I had the town's defences modernised by Girolamo Marini, who he put in charge of fortifying Vitry-le-François. The site was taken Condé during the Fronde in 1652, and re-taken by Louis XIV himself in 1653. The young Pérignon, who was born here in 1633, had already left family for the Benedictines. The houses were half-timbered, in the Champagne style. A fire in 1719 destroyed the entire town, and Monsieur de Force, the king's engineer, rebuilt it to a strict plan, in Champagne bond, alternating Gaize stone and brick, giving the whole town an interesting unit During the night of the 20 to 21 June 1791, Louis XVI and his family fled hastily away in a berlin in an attempt to reach Metz. They were recognis by the son of the postmaster at the hamlet of Chaintrix, then at Châlons; the news spread rapidly; after passing through Ste. Ménéhould, everyone kn that the king had just gone through. Jean-Baptiste Drouet, son of the Post master, rode at full gallop, taking short-cuts through the Argonne, to staging post at Varennes and had the king arrested on the Aire bridge. So as not to spill the blood of his people, the king refused to allow his hussars release him. Drouet had a successful career, and was sub-prefect of Ste Ménéhould from 1800 to 1814.

Place of the Hôtel-de-vil

ROYES. The Gauls of Tricasses, settled in the Seine and Aube valleys in that area before they join, to the south of the territories inhabited by e Remi and the Catalauni, with the Senones to the west and the Lingones to the east as neighbours, established a stronghold between some anches of the Seine, in an area of marshland and small islands. The Romans built a town here that they called Augustobona, after the holy title Augustus used by the emperors. The foundations of buildings belonging to a late first century town have been discovered, without ramparts, for X ROMANA reigned. The town, on the Roman road from Lyons to Reims, benefited from a flow of trade, which, over the centuries, it was to uggle to retain or control.

ter the shock of the first invasions by the Franks, the Burgundians and the Vandals, in 275 it reverted to its original name, Tricassium Civitas, or y of the Tricasses, gradually transformed in the Romanic language (late vulgar Latin) into Troyes.

the 6th century, part of the Frankish kingdom of Reims, its territory was then annexed to Burgundy, while Reims and Châlons had stronger links th Frankia. In 451, Attila and his people, the Huns, pillaged Troyes, and according to some authors, spared it. The legend of Saint-Loup, the wn's bishop, has it that having left the protection of its walls and armed only with his faith, he demanded to be taken to the king who he won er with his charisma and persuaded to divert his hordes. This is not unlikely, the young Attila had spent some years at the court of the Byzantine peror as a hostage, guarantor of treaties between his uncle Rua and the emperor. Educated amongst Christians, he spoke Greek and probably tin. In the Carolingian period there is reliable evidence of an

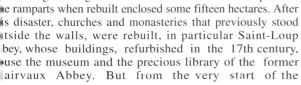

tive market in Troyes. In the 9th century, the town, capital of county, was already endowed with many churches, abbeys d trading establishments within the city walls, protected by e abundant waters of the branches of the Seine and its butary, the Vienne. At the end of the 9th century however, the wing waters also brought to its gates barges carrying rmans who sacked and burned it, devastating the area rrounding the religious demesnes, the hamlets and crops. e ramparts when rebuilt enclosed some fifteen hectares. After s disaster, churches and monasteries that previously stood tside the walls, were rebuilt, in particular Saint-Loup bey, whose buildings, refurbished in the 17th century, use the museum and the precious library of the former airvaux Abbey. But from the very start of the

10th century, its life force carried it to new heights, invasions were forgotten, the town developed new districts outside the walls to the south-west where Saint-Remi church was constructed, later followed by Saint-Urbain, Saint-Etienne, Sainte-Madeleine, Saint-Jean-au-Marché, Saint-Pantaléon and Saint-Nicolas. The Counts of Troyes settled in their town and by the north west corner of the first city wall erected their keep and castle, demolished in the 19th century. In the 11th and 12th centuries, the town continued to grow in several stages towards the east. The town walls, often made from earthworks armed with palisades and bordered by moats fed from the Seine or the Vienne, extended around the new districts, enclosing the new abbey and monastery parishes of Saint-Nizier, Saint-Martin-es-Aires and Saint-Denis. The half-timbered houses were similar to those that can still be seen in the old town, but thatched with straw, rushes, or tight bundles of reeds. These materials, wood and thatch, caused Troyes to fall prey to terrible fires on several occasions as it did in 1138. The most destructive, in 1524, devoured a quarter of the buildings but they were quickly rebuilt by the merchants of Troyes (some owned dozens of houses) in the traditional style with touches of Renaissance taste. From this last phase of development date many of the Champagne town houses of which Troyes presents the largest and most evocative group.

It was Count Henri the Liberal who made Troyes the county town of Champagne. Succeeding his father Thibaud II in 1152 he left his fiefs of Loire and Beauce to his younger brothers and vassals taking the title Count of Troyes. He earned the nickname Liberal or Generous because of his largesse and generosity, having numerous churches built in Champagne, including Saint-Etienne de Troyes and the hôtel-Dieu (hospital), close to his new residence in the south west corner of the walled town, that he preferred to the austere keep of his forefathers.

His wife, Marie de France, daughter of Louis VII and Alienor, inspired a court of literary figures, poets and musicians where the

Above, half-timbered houses with cob walls and projecting upper storeys.
Left, Rue des Chats, whose houses lean so far towards those facing them, they almost touch.

illustrious Chrétien de Troyes, author of «Launcelot or the Knight of the Cart» and «Percival or the Story of the Grail», shone. His heroes, through a thousand details regarding their customs, dress and attitudes bring the people of Troyes, great and small, and their world, back to life.

Thibaud IV of Champagne, grandson of Count Henri was himself to be the great 13th century poet of northern France.

For two centuries under the sovereign counts, Troyes enjoyed opulence with the institution of fairs, including two at Troyes, the «foire chaude» on 24 June, and the «foire froide» on the 1 or 2 November, each lasting about two months. The town was filled to overflowing with goods, cloth, precious fabrics and silks, spices, weapons, leather goods, horses and mules, wine, silver and gold ware, coins and money bills - trade in which was the exclusive province of Lombards and Florentines. The entire town lived on the fair which was held around the church of St-Jean-au-Marché.

Champagne itself became French in the 14th century. Paris tempted the commercial traffic away and the fairs of Troyes became regional. The last Italian financiers left their mansions in 1350.

But the bourgeois of Troyes continued to produce goods. They developed their industry, tanneries and leather workshops, paper mills turned by the Seine and its canals, inside and outside the town, and finally hosiery, whose entrepreneurs bought and ordered from the country people, in the market halls of Troyes, well before they set up their own workshops. This last activity, despite war, revolution and changes of régime has continued to expand until our own times, becoming the industry most representative of the Troyes area.

In 1367 king Charles V had the town fortified under the guidance of a council of bourgeois put in charge of supervising the work and providing a significant proportion of the finance. They were, in addition, to maintain the works and form a defensive militia. Stone walls and towers were erected, ditches were dug, the faubourgs outside the walls were razed to the ground. The militias trained in archery and the use of crossbows. The site of Troyes remained

impregnable. In 1368 Charles V appointed his brother, the duke of Burgundy, Philip the Bold, his lieutenant in Champagne. The duke often stayed in Troyes. He died there in 1404 of the first plague of this terrible century which saw ten epidemics, wiping out 75% of the population.

It was in Troyes on 21 May 1420 that the treaty was signed under whose terms Henry V, king of England, claimed the throne of France by marrying Catherine, daughter of Charles VI, the Mad, and Isabeau, who denied Charles, the Dauphin and called the Englishman her son. Troyes eradicated this stain by opening its gates in July 1429, after negotiations with the bishop Jean Léguisé, to the army of Charles VII and Joan of Arc, on their way to Reims. One imagines that Joan and the Dauphin, received by the bishop, were taken to pray in the cathedral. Constructed after the fire of 1188, with work starting about 1200, and continuing until the 16th century, and with the chancel constructed first, it would have reached the first bays of the nave by the late 13th century. A series of disasters and collapses marked the 14th century, the rose window of the north transept and the vaulting of part of the nave fell down. In 1429 restoration work on the church was still in progress. Work continued until the early 16th century when the nave was completed. The façade was entrusted, in the first half of the 16th century, to the very distinguished architect, Chambiges, then to his pupils, including his son; Jean Bailly finished the clock floor. The left tower rose slowly to the small turrets featuring in every view of the town. From the 13th to the 16th century the cathedral of Saint-Pierre and Saint-Paul (the Saint-Paul tower was never built) reflects every period of Gothic style and elements of the principal cathedrals can be seen. The windows similarly trace the history of stained glass making from the 13th to 16th century.

Above, Mansion built either for Canon Budé, brother of the humanist Guillaume Budé, or for Odard Hennequin, bishop from 1527 to 1544.
Opposite, the cathedral chancel.

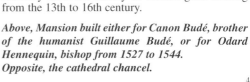

The misfortunes of a century of war, sackings, famines a
plagues had emptied the villages and fields. The poor wander
in the forests or took refuge in the towns. Troyes, in about 148
had approximately 15,000 inhabitants within its walls and 3,0
paupers begging their bread, on the margins of society and oft
ill tolerated. From the 15th century dates the theme of the dans
macabres [Dance of Death], of which wood engravings were to
printed in Troyes and distributed in the kingdom by pedlars w
carried a full range of popular literature - shepherds' calenda
legends and the lives of the saints and almanachs, which this tov
of papermakers was to make a speciality until the 19th century.

The people of Troyes were in fact to continue to be active
involved in industry and commerce and, after having rallied to t
support of Charles VII, they obtained royal protection maintain
by Louis XI, but without the commercial privileges they we
hoping for - the merchants of Paris were too near and t
powerful to tolerate that. So the people of Troyes put their effo
into their traditional industries, textiles, leather goods ar
shoemaking, paper goods and .... wine. Bishop Jean Légui
encouraged this enterprise and for his part endeavoured to refor
his clergy, to improve teaching, and opened schools in Troyes a
in the diocese.

In the reigns of Louis XII, Francis I and then Henry II, prosperi
continued to grow despite the war waged by Charles Quint
north Champagne. In 1511, the bourgeois obtained an open fa
for two weeks from 8 May, in 1524 a second two week fair on
October, but trade was subject to that of the Lyons' fairs whe
Troyes merchants went to buy a good part of their raw materi;
and imported items, silk and spices. The population increased
22,500 by the middle of the century, and the merchants of a fe
families from the elite of local society lived like the nob
seigneurs, such as the Mauroy family, who built, around 1560, o
of the largest private mansions of the Renaissance perio
comprising an inner courtyard within four wings, mostly ha
timbered, with some parts of the structure in stone, columns
the portal of the main façade, and built mainly of stone and bri
laid in a chessboard pattern. The builder's wife bequeathed h
home to found the Trinité orphanage. At the end of the 18
century these buildings housed the first specialist hosiery facto;
whose machinery, which was to become universal, at first dealt
blow to the men and women workers who knitted by hand both
the town and on the farms.

Between the late 15th century and the Wars of Religion, tl
numerous churches unfinished, for lack of men or lack of mone
in a town of which it was said that the bells never stopp
answering each other, the disastrous fire of 1524 and tl
economic recovery gave the artisans of Troyes, carpente;

Opposite, staircase tower of the Mauroy mansion, now a museum
tools, workers' literature and trade guilds.
Above, galleries on the upper floors of a mansion of tradition
design overlook a courtyard.

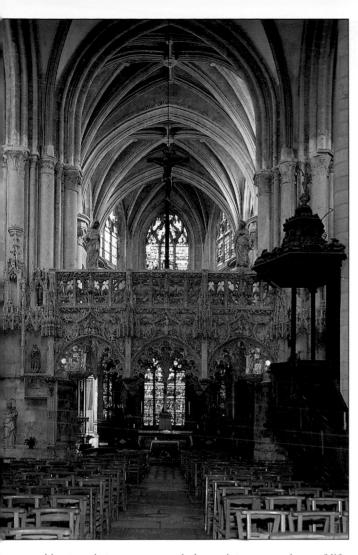

Opposite: Sainte-Madeleine, Jean Gaide's rood screen.
Above: Sainte Madeleine (Master of the Sainte-Madeleine church).
Below: West front of St-Urbain.

it, resembling the miniatures with which monks decorated manuscripts, so ethereal, light and airy are its lines, unconstrained by the law of gravity. And, just as in the illuminated manuscripts we see demons attempting their evil enterprises, the monk could well have portrayed the abbess of the nearby Notre-Dame convent, who had the chancel sacked in order to prevent its planned consecration in 1266, sabotaging a church encroaching on her domain and beyond her authority. After the Pope's death in 1264, his nephew, Cardinal Ancher, had undoubtedly offended the sensibilities of the ambitious nun. Subsequently, there was a fire, perhaps deliberate, and it was later noticed that the donations had been misappropriated. The cardinal died and Saint-Urbain remained unfinished until the works undertaken in the 19th century to save and complete the building to the original plans, a marvel of grace and lightness.

sons, architects and stone carvers and glass painters a new lease of life, piring them, in a continuity of Gothic style and the discovery of the naissance, a distinctive Troyes school style, combining modest simplicity h a mastery and elegance worthy of the greatest.

masterpiece and excellent example of this Troyes school is the Sainte rthe in Sainte-Madeleine church, in the right arm of the transept, the pression of the unity of body and soul, of the divine and the human, hout dramatisation, unemphatically, with grave and sustained simplicity.

nte-Madeleine, founded in the 12th century and rebuilt in the 13th, was vided in the early 16th century with a new chancel in the flamboyant le and a rood screen, still in place, although this liturgical separation has n removed in most churches. This was constructed by Jean Gaide, an hitect and parishioner, with the help of the sculptor Nicolas Halins, ther well-known artist representative of the Troyes school. The stained ss windows, the work of named local glass painters, also testify to the stic revival of the period.

signed between 1260 and 1270 by the master builder Jean Langlois, int-Urbain church is also a masterpiece of the spirit and poetic agination which has always counterbalanced the practical and material look of the people of Troyes, whether merchant or poet, or both.

e history of Saint-Urbain seems the stuff of gilded Legend, «Once upon a e ....» there was a modest shoemaker (one of the commonest occupations the town) called Pantaléon, whose son, Jacques Pantaléon, was noticed the priests who taught him, was a brilliant student and became bishop of rdun and patriarch of Jerusalem. There were at that time many people m Champagne in the Holy Land. Finally, elected Pope as Urban IV, he ated a considerable sum to found, as an act of grace, a collegiate church the place where his father's cobbler's shop once stood, that he bought ether with the necessary ground. He dedicated the church to Saint ban, the Champagne-born Pope and preacher of the First Crusade.

his true story seems miraculous, the church is a miraculous illustration of

Above: «Le Rapt», a sculpture by Suchetet, Préfectu[re] gardens.
Opposite: the Vauluisant mansion, residence of the abbot[s] Vauluisant, sold in the 15th century, destroyed by fire [in] 1524, purchased by Antoine Hennequin and reconstruc[ted] around 1564 although its twin towers seem to date from [the] 15th century. The mansion houses two museums, one of [Art] and History, and the other devoted to hosiery.

The Troyes school of sculpture, that of Sainte Marthe, [the] entombments of Chaource and Bayel, Saint Peter and Sa[int] Martin bronzes conserved by the cathedral treasure-hou[se] interested the great Italian artists of the Fontaineble[au] School, Le Rosso and Le Primatice. The latter received [the] benefice of the Troyes abbey of St-Martin-es-Aires fr[om] Francis I and worked at Polisy château, near Bar-sur-Sei[ne] for the Dinteville family. His pupil, the Florenti[ne] Domenico del Barbiere, called «Dominique Florenti[n»] settled in Troyes in about 1540 and was successful the[re] directing the art of Troyes to a degree of mannerism, w[ith] more technique and less soul, but vigorous. In [the] flamboyant style, Renaissance, St-Pantaléon chur[ch] several of his works can be seen together with other wo[rks] of the first Troyes school, whose masters rema[in] anonymous, and from the second, his own and that of [his] disciples, including François Gentil and Julyot.

It was at the same period that the religious conflict of the Reformation took shape. Troyes, at first relatively tolerant, had three pastors in 1561, with congregations of several hundred faithful, including both common people and local worthies. The Catholic bishop, Antonio Carraciolo, motivated by an ecumenical spirit, undertook to reconcile the two sides in a joint reform, but Catholic and Reformist extremists and rival political ambitions, did not allow him to succeed. He was replaced in 1562 by a more orthodox prelate. Many Protestant families took refuge abroad, at least those whose fortunes permitted it, after the Wassy massacre in 1562 and that of St-Barthélémy in August 1572 (when thirty-seven reformists were massacred in the prisons), and lastly, after the occupation of Troyes by the Leaguers. The town, royalist until 1588, passed into the hands of the extremist Leaguers and only yielded to Henry IV after his renunciation [of Protestantism] and coronation in 1594.

Spanish wars under Louis XIII, the Fronde under the Regency of Anne of Austria and Louis XIV's war against the Duke of Lorraine, devastated Champagne, a frontier province until the conquest of Alsace by Louis XIV and Lorraine by Louis XV. As always, it was the flat land that suffered and Troyes was filled with all those fleeing the miseries of the War, so accurately portrayed by the Lorraine engraver, Jacques Callot. This prolific craftsman worked for the entrepreneurs of Troyes, tanners and paper-makers, and especially the hosiery makers, some of whom used dozens of different looms and employed up to 500 workers in the town or the villages, increasing the gap between the bourgeoisie and the often miserable common people. The revolution accentuated this gap and money became the leading factor in the 19th century. In 1797 the municipality wanted to demolish all the churches except the cathedral. The Directoire very fortunately prevented this disaster being inflicted on most of them. St-Remi (14th C), St-Nicolas (16th C), St-Jean (13th, 15th, 16th C), St-Nizier (16th C), St-Pantaléon (16th C), St-Urbain (13th C) and Ste-Madeleine (13th-16th C), have been left to us, still a fine litany.

The hosiery makers were then knitting the first fancy stockings for fashionable men and women. Men and dynasties would change, but the fortunes of hosiery would continue to our day.

Above, the old bishop's palace (16th-17th century), museum of Modern Art,

Top right, hanging turret room at the Marisy mansion (about 1530), rue Chardonnet.

Right, rue Champaux, house built for the silversmith Roize, started in 1578 and completed in 1618.

Opposite, page 46, bottom, the Haute-Seine canal, Préfecture gardens and Saint-Urbain church.

ORIENT FOREST REGIONAL NATURE RESERVE.

The 70,000 ha of protected land has led to cooperation between the fifty communes around the Orient forest and three large lakes to protect the natural environment, flora, fauna, countryside and the surroundings of local residents, and to ensure this heritage is explored in a regulated way so as not to upset this delicate balance.

The forest does not get its lovely name from its location about fifteen km east of Troyes, county town of Champagne, but from the commanderies and demesnes of the Order of the Knights Templar, whose duty was to protect pilgrims in the Christian orient of the Holy Places. The Order was founded in 1118 by Hughes de Payns, a knight of Champagne and seven other knights from Champagne and Flanders. Count Hugues de Champagne was himself to be made a knight templar in 1125. As both monk and knight, the templars accepted the Rule of St. Bernard, took part in all the crusades and were also bankers to the crusaders and pilgrims, from whom they received funds in France which would be available to them in the Orient, protecting them against robberies and losses during a perilous journey. The order became very powerful and very rich, its mistakes became crimes, its faults infamies. Philip the Fair, in 1307, used this as a pretext to suppress it at the end of an iniquitous procedure, causing men to perish and depriving them of their riches. The land and command posts of the Templars passed into the hands of the knights Hospitaliers of Saint-John of Jerusalem. The aura of mystery associated with the brilliant and dark history of these soldier monks, the legend of their buried treasure and their secret rituals still hovers over their former estates.

The lakes were created by the Institution Interdépartementale des Barrages Réservoirs [regional reservoir authority] of the Seine basin, to control the distribution of the waters of the Seine and the Aube in the heart of the rich wooded countryside of wetland Champagne, where waters, from time immemorial, have run in streams, lingered in pools and marshes, rising beneath the fields and roots, even beneath the château of Vendeuvre ... «... remarkable for its antiquity, it is situated on a rock surrounded by beautiful large gardens ... facing a fine park. The source of the river Barse can be seen emerging from beneath the château building, giving such a great abundance of water that it turns several watermills a few toises from the source» [a toise is about 2 metres or 6» feet] as Mr. Denis, a geographer, described it in 1770 in his description of the route from Troyes to Langres, pointing out rich prairies, willows, poplar groves, fountains and fish ponds everywhere along the road, indications of the abundance of water.

The first lake, and the most southerly, Orient lake, is a reservoir of the Seine and came into service in 1966. It covers 2,300 ha. Three sandy beaches, Lusigny-sur-Barse, Géraudot and Mesnil-Saint-Père, have been provided with facilities for bathing, sun-bathing and watching sailing boats of all classes competing with each other. Private motor boats are not permitted.

In the area north-east of this first lake, the Morge des Bois pool has been laid out as a bird sanctuary, overlooked by the Maison du Parc, with the game observation ground. Wildlife can be observed from either.

In 1990 and 1991 two tributary lakes regulating the

course of the Aube came into service.

The Temple lake, 2000 hectares of peaceful waters, is dedicated to peace and tranquillity. Small craft row over the water (electrically driven boats are permitted), carrying fisherman and nature watchers across the shimmering sheet of liquid mirror. Long pike lie in wait, at an angle, noses to the surface, or slumber between the currents, sated, noses to the bottom. White fish, flashes of silver, ricochet over the water, fleeing the striped perch; shoals of round-backed carp graze on underwater pastures, then kiss the surface or sleep, wedged beneath the banks. You can see fat dark tench with golden sides.

In the shallower waters of the sloping banks, banks of young fish of every kind move ceaselessly, darting here and there in search of food. The countless, secret world of aquatic insects is intimately bound to that of fish, amphibians and birds.

More than 265 species of birds share the skies, fields, trees and waters, raptors, web-footed and passerines, and twice a year, the great migrating species. Grey cranes, harvest geese, egrets, mute swans with their singing wings, every type of duck, divers, widgeon, teal, and the occasional fish-eating eagle, which has a bigger wingspan than the golden eagle, can be seen here. When, in early Spring, the large flocks pass over our countryside

turning to the north and east of Europe, and on their return at grape-picking time, it can truthfully be said that they are coming, or have just come r a short holiday on the great lakes of the Champagne area.

ake Amance, further east, has as its main centre Port-Dienville, and reserves 500 of its 700 hectares for motorised water sports of all kinds - water-kiing, jet-skiing, hovercraft and Γ 3000s set official records here each spring.

here is one beach, however, well away from the bustle and the noisy boat lanes, in its own part of the lake so that swimmers can bathe in peace. his ingenious division of activities between the three lakes prevents conflict between sailing, rowing and motor boat enthusiasts. Those alert to he sounds of nature are assured of the necessary quiet, high-speed motor craft do not have to worry about cutting fragile sailing boats in two or earing the idling dinghy of a dozing fisherman.

Bronze fish on the dyke at Lake Amance; sculptors Silvia Lacaisse and Patrice Alexandre. Cast by Fonderies G.H.M. Sommevoire.

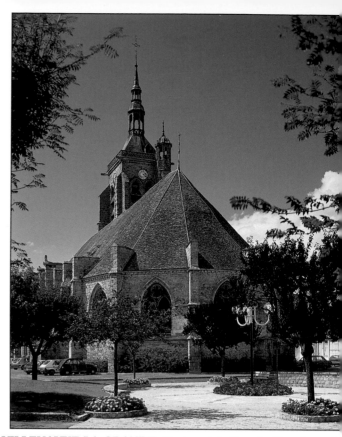

NOGENT-SUR-SEINE. In the 9th century, Saint-Denis abbey had land and watermills here. The mills were working until 1990. The flamboyant chancel and transept of St-Laurent's church were rebuilt under Henri II, to form, with the Nemours palace, now demolished, a group of second Renaissance buildings.

VILLENAUXE-LA-GRANDE. The town is built on the Noxe from wh it takes its name. The road from Troyes to Meaux was used from the century by convoys of merchants, escorted at the times of the Champagne fa by county sergeants. The church of St-Pierre and St-Paul, with its triple na was built of local sandstone in the 13th and 16th centuries.

ROMILLY-SUR-SEINE. The industrial town, specialising in the manufacture of the hosiery, breeches and stockings shown on its coat of arms, honoured with a long history. The Romans named it, Attila passed through it, Saint Geneviève came here by boat in 484, to seek grain for Parisians. It has lived through all the joys and misfortunes of France. Voltaire, too, was brought here by carriage in early June 1778, dead, afte post-mortem, sewn up again, dressed and held by a valet so the body didn't fall off, his face seemed to be laughing as he was taken to the convent Sellières by his nephew, Mignot, the abbot, who had him buried here in defiance of the Church.

AR-SUR-SEINE. The counts of Tonnerre then of Brienne owned the seigniory in the 11th and 12th centuries. It passed, through marriage, the du Puiset family which was wiped out during the crusade to Damiette in Egypt (1249). Jeanne de Navarre, countess of Champagne, born Bar in 1273, married Philip the Fair in 1284, and Bar became part of the kingdom of France.

ring the Hundred Years War, the town, prize of the battle between France and Burgundy, was destroyed in 1359 by Brocart de Fénétrange, a rraine mercenary of the Anglo-Burgundians who boasted of having laid waste 900 wealthy estates. It was rebuilt fairly quickly, as is the vilege of timber-built towns, but had to be ceded to Philip the Good, duke of Burgundy, as part of the Treaty of Arras (1435). Charles Amboise retook it in 1475, for Louis XI.

Bar-sur-Seine, in the midst of vines

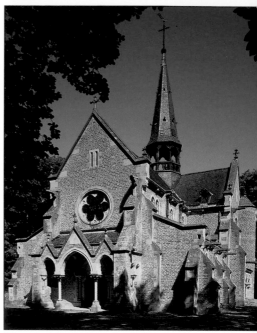

Chapel of Notre-Dame du Chêne

Huguenots and Catholics fought over it in 1562, 1591 and 1592. It surrendered to Henri IV in 1594 and demolished its walls. The king havi￼
granted the fiefdom to the Bourbon-Montpensier family, their daughter married Gaston d'Orléans, brother of Louis XIII. Their daughter, Ann￼
Marie, duchess of Montpensier, known as the Grande Mademoiselle, took a crazily active part in the Fronde.

In 1814, the king of Prussia, the Tzar and the emperor of Austria, successively established their headquarters at Bar-sur-Seine.

A few of the vaults in the lower parts of the château testify to this historic past, as do some fine 15th and 16th century half-timbered houses, t￼
church of St-Etienne, constructed between the early 16th and the beginning of the 17th century in the gothic style, except for the portal dated 161￼
the capitals of the nave and the Renaissance stained-glass windows, coloured, greys and silvery yellows. Bar-sur-Seine is also a well-known wir￼
growing area, surrounded by vines in rows on the hillsides, the roofs of the town look like an ordinary village of wine-growers.

CHAOURCE. Henri the Liberal emancipated the commune in 1165, which thereafter shared t￼
history of south Champagne. The church of St-Jean-Baptiste (13th - 16th century) of t￼
«champenoise hall» type houses, in the last chapel on the left, the entombment given in 1515 ￼
Nicolas de Monstier, captain of Chaource, and by his wife; the work of the Master of Chaource a￼
known as the Master of Ste Marthe expresses the drama of the Passion with that same simplicit￼
contained emotion, a sense of the sacred - you can almost hear the sublime music of the Passio￼
composed by Bach two centuries later.

Amadys Jamin, born in Chaource in 1538, secretary to Ronsard and then poet to Charles IX, returned to ￼
birthplace and died there in about 1585. Art and poetry should not lead the visitor to neglect the tr￼
«Chaource» - a creamy cheese, produced from the herds grazing on the lush fields seen all around the tow￼

AR-SUR-AUBE. The town grew out of the ...aulish and later Gallo-Roman stronghold, Segessera, ...mmanding the Aube and the Agrippa Way from Italy ... England from the Sainte-Germaine promontory. ...e site owes its name to Germaine, martyred by the ...andals who razed the city in the 5th century. A cross ...d a chapel commemorate her sacrifice.

...e château was reconstructed in the early ...erovingian period on the Sainte-Germaine hillside. ... the 12th century, the count abandoned the heights to ...uild a new stronghold on the Aube, enabling it to ...ow, under his authority, into a bustling town enclosed ... solid walls, trading in woollens, cloths, glassware ...d wines.

... the late 11th century, Thibaud I, having married the ...ountess Adèle de Bar, brought the seigniory into the ...ounty of Champagne. In 1190, Thibault II instigated ...e annual cycle of Champagne fairs. Bar proclaimed ...e fair open from the feast of Sainte-Germaine on 29 ...ugust, and it lasted to the end of October, after the ...ape harvest, attracting traders in woollen cloth, ...ather and other goods from a good proportion of ...urope, then the bankers, Florentines and Lombards. ...or a long time one street bore the name rue des ...ngoisselles; after the Anguisolli, bankers, who had a

...ansion and banking hall here. When Champagne became French its commercial and financial trade was absorbed by Paris. The fairs became big ...gional markets. The town, however, was wealthy and its bourgeois had obtained a charter and freedoms from Count Thibaut IV in around 1232. Bar ...en experienced, like the entire kingdom, wars and miseries, until our times. From the bridge that preceded the present Aube bridge, Charles VII had ...e bastard of Bourbon, chief of the mercenaries who were terrorising the region, drowned. A chapel on the bridge commemorated the execution. ...he fortified walls, the château, the old bridge and the chapel and most of the pre-16th century civil buildings have disappeared, but the churches have ...reserved the memories of the old walled town. Saint-Maclou church, created from the castle chapel, still identifiable in the ...entre of the chancel, donated to the Benedictines in 1076, then by Count Henri-le-Large to a college of canons in 1160, was ...nlarged in the late 12th century. The apse and apsidals date from the 14th century; the bell-tower is a legacy of the château ...hose keep it was. The façade (1740) was inspired by the entrance to the cloister at Clairvaux, then recently rebuilt. ...aint-Pierre church, built in the 11th and 12th centuries, is marked by the sober style of Citeaux and Clairvaux. The façade and ...e right side as far as the bell tower were preceded by a 14th century wooden gallery, a covered walk known as «The Halloy». ...he 16th, 17th and 18th century houses are reminders of the rebuilding work after the disasters of wars. Their basements retain ...ome fine cellars, wine cellars and warehouses from the days of the great fairs. At No. 26 rue du Général Vouillemont,

there remains a house belonging to Clairvaux abbey, a monks' hostel, a vaulted wine and provisions storeroom and 12th century storage rooms.
Three leagues from Bar, on 25 June 1115, the Benedictine monk Bernard Tescelin de Saure, son of the lord of Fontaine, near Dijon, arrived from Citeaux abbey with twelve companions and settled in the Absinthe vale that they called «Clair Val», an estate donated by Hugues, the count of Champagne. He later became Saint Bernard, the most influential person in all domains in the Europe of his day. The abbey was to prosper, playing an important economic role throughout the region until the Revolution, creating in the 14th century, a group of metal works south-east of Chaumont, which made the leading iron producer in Champagne. The abbey church was destroyed during the Revolution. Napoleon made the abbey a penitentiary.

BRIENNE-LE-CHATEAU. Of the keep of the Brienne house nothing remains. The counts distinguished themselves in all the battles and in the Holy Land itself, where there were great many men from Champagne. Jean de Brienne fought beside the kings Philip-Augustus and Richard of England. He married Marie, heiress of the king and queen of Jerusalem; king from 1210 to 1225, dethroned by his son-in-law, Frederick II, emperor of Germany, he became regent-emperor of Constantinople from 1231 to 1237. Erard de Brienne took the cross in his turn, with Count Thibaud V, the king St.-Louis and lord of Joinville, another Champagne man, who was to tell the story of their campaigns in his old age. The last of the line, Gautier VI, constable of France, was killed in Poitiers in 1356. The land passed to the Enghien family of Luxembourg, and was then sold in 1634 to Louis XIII's Secretary of State, Loménie. The present château was built by Fontaine between 1770 and 1778 for Louis de Loménie, brother of Louis XVI's minister.
The church, refurbished in the 16th century, has retained a few parts of the 12th century building, where the future king of Jerusalem and emperor of Constantinople, then Count Erard, companion to Saint Louis were baptised. Another future emperor, Napoleon Bonaparte, made his first communion

here, and was accepted on 25th April 1779, at the Royal Military School. He left on 30 October 1784, highly thought of, for the Royal Military School in Paris. What were his feelings in Brienne in 1814, at the head of his troops, so glorious only a short while before, as they retreated step by step, harassed by the allies, still winning victories, and so close to farewells? The collection of memorabilia in a small museum at his former college is an invitation to reflect on this extraordinary destiny.

CIREY-SUR-BLAISE. As one who had supported the Fronde, the marquis of Châtelet saw his château razed to the ground in 1633. Pardonned, he rebuilt half of it ten years later. The lower wing against the unfinished gable end, was fitted out by Voltaire when he stayed there, between 1734 and 1749, with Madame du Châtelet, his mistress, the beautiful Emilie, an intellectual, physician, philosopher and a very liberated woman. The biddable marquis liked Voltaire. Perhaps he was content to continue the work and cover a ground floor started in the 17th century. The apartments were «comfortable» (Voltaire had lived in England) with a luxurious bathroom, often described, and a small theatre under the eaves. Above the entrance, decorated with shells and symbols of the arts and sciences, a Latin inscription recalls the couple's leisure activities. «Deus nobis haec otia faecit», «A god made this retreat for us». Emilie died in childbirth in 1749 after a love affair with the poet St-Lambert, and with her loss Voltaire lost Cirey, replacing it ten years later with the château of Ferney.

COLOMBEY-LES-DEUX-EGLISES. The Blaise runs between the villages towards the Marne which it joins after Vitry. Upstream of Cirey, it flows at the foot of the Colombey hills, within walking distance of the Boisserie where General de Gaulle lived - one landscape evoking two famous men who could not be more dissimilar.

Charles de Gaulle, who made Colombey his Ferney, did not want a court here, but a somewhere to think, to enable him to rise above the commonplace, far from the «tumult of men and events», in the family home, close to nature, marked by generations of peasant farmers, in a

...ple village. He wrote, thought, entertained a few of the faithful, always concerned for France, occupied by the essential. The death he ...aited came on 9th November 1970, at home, thirteen days before his eightieth birthday. His tomb in the village cemetery bears the inscription ...wanted, CHARLES DE GAULLE (1890-1970). The rest, his life as a soldier, politician and statesman, his titles, his victories and his defeats, ...ong to History, but the Boisserie allows us a discreet glimpse of his daily life.

...posite page, top, the château at Cirey; Below, above the woods, the Memorial cross (1972 - designed by M. Nébinger - M. Mosser).
...ove: La Boisserie, from the garden - Below: the church of Colombey (12th and 16th centuries).

SAINT-DIZIER. Olonna, inhabited by Celtic iron-masters then a Gallo-Roman metal working centre, used iron from local mines. The walled town, abandoned in the second century, was repopulated in the next. In about 260 Christians are said to have taken refuge here with the relics of St.-Didier, and the town took his name. This important place on the Eastern frontier was still well-fortified. In 1544, Charles Quint with 50,000 men, only took it after six weeks. Calamities, wars and a fire in 1775 have destroyed most of the historic buildings. Of Notre-Dame, St.-Martin de la Noue and Gigny church, however, there remains a façade, a tower or a portal, evidence of their former glories.

MONTIER-EN-DER. In 650, Saint Berchaire, co-founder of Hautvillers abbey, having retired to the forest of Der, was joined by his disciples and founded the monastery in Der, Monstier-en-Der, obedient to the rule of St. Colomban, on an estate donated by Childéric II. Adson, abbot from 960 to 982, and distinguished author of the treatise on the Antichrist, built the church which was consecrated before the first millennium. The great arcades of the nave remain, reconstructed after the fire of 1940. The façade and side aisles date from the early 11th century; the chancel, ambulatory and transept are early 13th century in the purity of early Gothic.

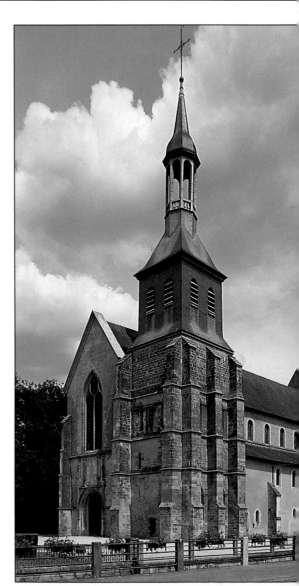

ER-CHANTECOQ LAKE. Before Der-Chantecoq lake was filled with water in 1974, Champagne countryside, an area of ancient forests, springs and streams, extended over th Marne and North Haute-Marne reaching to the edge of the North-East of the Aube.

e Blaise and the Marne used to overflow in periods of spate, their waters rushing controllably towards the Seine and Paris, causing catastrophic floods several times in each tury.

vas to control these winter spates of the two rivers and provide a water supply for the isian region that the 650 hectare Champaubert reservoir was first constructed, later ended to the present 4,800 hectares, with 77 km of banks around the perimeter. The eloper was the Institution Interdépartementale des Barrages Réservoirs du Bassin de la ne. The work resulted in three villages vanishing beneath the waters, Chantecoq, isement and Champaubert. Champaubert church remained, sole survivor of the village, on ngue of land above the waters of the lake. Nuisement church was rebuilt at Sainte-Marie-Lac. Of Chantecoq, one small island remains, the top of the hill on whose sides the age was built.

e whole of the eastern part of the lake, one of the largest in Europe, seems rooted in the est of Der, cut into small coves, estuaries of streams and channels, jagged creeks and dflats, while the main basin stretches out westwards between more regular banks.

e forest of Der, which comes from the Celtic word for oak tree, was for a long time the g's domain, owned by the count during the period of independent Champagne, both made ations to the abbeys that wished to settle here. One part that belonged to the lords of ville later became the property of the house of Lorraine, and then of its youngest branch, Guise family, and finally, returned to the house of Orleans.

e lake and forest make up an experimental ecosystem in a wetland area, that the local orities and environmental groups have successfully balanced, despite constraints associated h the periodic retention and release of the waters, creating variations in water level. merous species of fish, amphibious creatures, such as frogs and toads, and aquatic insects ed prolifically and large numbers of lake and marshland birds can be seen here, wild

e 60, top, St.-Dizier: le Jard - Chevet of Gigny church.
om: Abbey church of Montier-en-Der. The monastery buildings, destroyed during the Revolution, e been replaced by the facilities of the Haras National [French national equine stud farm]
w: the Champaubert peninsula.

ans, ducks, geese, waders, mudflat feeders, permanent residents
d especially migrant species, like grey cranes, who have now
ade the Der a regular Autumn and late Winter port of call. Here
o, can be seen fish-eating birds of prey swooping and skimming
er the golden plumes of reedbeds, large almost submerged
rmorants, heads on periscopes, diving lengthily and reappearing
expectedly.

an, in the shape of walkers, ramblers, sailing enthusiasts,
noeists and rowers, even of less environmentally friendly water
orts, learns to respect the flora and fauna on this lake which is a
luable educational resource. The same approach is possible all
und the lake, particularly in the forest. While, on the water,
glers fish, sailors tack in their boats, hold regattas or return to
eir home port at Nuisement, Nemours or Giffaumont, landlubbers
le, walk or cycle exploring the natural environment, fascinated by
untry crafts, the world of bees or visit the barn-like churches of
nampagne, Bailly-le-Franc, Outines, Châtillon-sur-Broué,
uisement, Arrigny, Lentilles, Drosnay and many others.

*posite page: The church formerly at Nuisement-aux-Bois, a typical
ampagne church, half-timbered and cob built, in the shape of a
rn. It was said that the Lord took more pleasure in this than in
ny cathedrals. It was dismantled when the village was to be flooded
d reconstructed in the neighbouring parish of Sainte-Marie.
mber frame buildings of this type, both houses and barns, were often
smantled and moved, being treated by notaries [conveyancing
icitors] as moveable assets.*

CHARLEVILLE-MEZIERES. Louis de Gonzague, third son of the duke of Mantoue, had acquired through his marriage to Henriette de Clèves, in 1565, the duchy of Nevers and the county of Rethel, in the kingdom of France. On his death, in 1595, his son Charles, following his father's example, who had assured the prosperity of Nevers by introducing the glass making, enamelling and art pottery industries, wished to give the county of Rethel a commercial boost by creating a new town here, to which first Henri IV then Louis XIII, his cousins, granted tax exemptions and franchises.

In 1606, Charles was 26 years of age and decided to found his town, Charleville, on the site of the small village of Arches, in a loop of the Meuse, on the left bank, facing fortified Mézières in the curve upstream, on the right bank.

From 1606 to 1608, he bought land and signed contracts with builders. The concept of the original plan is attributed to several architects and engineers, Moreau, the engraver of the plan published by Mérian in 1646, Clément Métézeau, younger brother of Louis, the king's engineer, to whom la place Royale in Paris (now place des Vosges) is attributed. Others suggest Claude Chastillon, the king's architect, responsible for a great many sites in the North and East. In any event, it was Clément Métézeau who completed the project selected. It is an example of original and innovative town planning, compared to other designs of the time, neither a town laid out in straight lines or a symmetrical grid pattern, like Richelieu, nor a fortified walled town. Six squares defined six districts - the ducal square at the

centre with the palace on the West side and the houses we see today on the other three sides. Behind the palace is a second service square, la place de Nevers. In the north-east district, overlooking the Meuse, is la place du St-Sépulcre, a priory of the order of the Christian Militia, created by the duke with the intention of retaking Constantinople from the Turks, for his ancestors had been emperors of it, (from 1683 the Turks were halted before Vienna by Jean Sobieski, and were, little by little, to be chased out of Europe). Place St-Ignace, in the north-west district, is the site of the village of Arches; in the south-west corner, the square where the Notre-Dame cathedral was later built; and finally, in the south-east district, la place St-François. All that was built in the 17th century repeats the type of house typical of the reigns of Henri IV and Louis XIII. The ducal square, 126 m long and 90 m wide, presents the ideal composition of the style. Each long side, north and south, is formed from ten houses, five on each side of the central street leading to the gates. Each group of five is itself formed from groups of two large stone and brick houses over arcades each with four bays, supporting two floors and a slate roof in the form known as «en pavillon», in the centre stands a single house with two bays supporting three floors, crowned, according to the initial plans, with a domed roof in the «imperial» style. The four-bayed houses comprise two residences, separated by a passageway giving access to the shops beneath the gallery of the arcades; for the builder wished to create a trading town. On the short East side, three double houses stand on each side of the central street. The intersecting main streets that divide the square also divide the town; rue Ste Catherine, from the Porte de France, in the South, to the seigniorial mill in the North, on the Meuse, a building of noble design but nonetheless functional: its wheels beneath the arches supplied the town with flour and the fountains with gushing water.

The ducal square [la place ducale] and the statue of Charles de Gonzague.

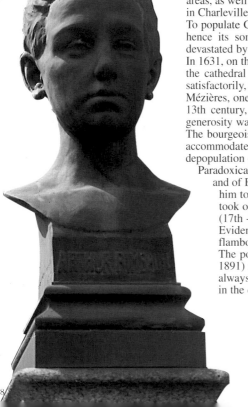

On the other bank, a fort crowns the summit of Mont Olympe. The main street crossing the first at a right angle, rue St-Charles, links the Flanders Gate [Porte de Flandre] in the west, to the Luxembourg gate.

In order to accomplish such a major financial project, the duke invited the towns of the Rethelois and Nivernais areas, as well as those of Champagne, of which he was governor on the king's behalf, to build their own house in Charleville. Thus it is that some gates bear the name of the towns who contributed.

To populate Charleville, he made it an asylum town, assuring immunity for debtors, bankrupts and criminals, hence its somewhat questionable reputation at the period. Land was granted free of charge. Mézières, devastated by war and militarised to excess, was emptied and moved over the Meuse.

In 1631, on the Duke's death, who had won back the throne of Mantoue in 1627, work on the ducal palace and the cathedral had barely begun. They were never finished and the town hall of 1843 completes, not very satisfactorily, the architectural group.

Mézières, one of Charlemagne's fortresses, already commanded the Meuse and its traffic; enfranchised in the 13th century, the commune grew so that by the end of the 15th century it had 6000 inhabitants, whose generosity was exemplary in a time of urban selfishness, when faced with a flood of refugee peasant farmers. The bourgeois organised their reception and provided the funds needed to assure the survival of the victims accommodated at l'Hôtel-Dieu, until peace came and the return to their villages, thus preventing the depopulation of the rural areas of the region.

Paradoxically the decline of the town was brought about by its strategic value and the heroism of the garrison and of Bayard, who withstood the siege of Charles Quint from 30 August to 27 September 1521, forcing him to withdraw. The soldiers then ousted the merchants, the ruined districts were not rebuilt, a citadel took over a large part of the space inside the ramparts, followed by a royal military engineering school (17th - 18th century), the present prefecture.

Evidence of Mézières before Charleville, Notre-Dame, constructed in the mid 16th century in the flamboyant Gothic style, received in 1570, Charles IX and Elisabeth of Austria who were married there. The poet Arthur Rimbaud (born in Charleville on 20 October 1854, died in Marseilles, 10 November 1891) rebel and visionary, fleeing all over Europe and as far as the East, cut himself off completely, but always came back to his home town and never failed to keep in touch with his family, even from deep in the deserts of Ethiopia.

Above: Mézières, the basilica of Notre-Dame de l'Espérance (1491 - 1615).
Charleville, Place Winston-Churchill, formerly Place St-François, «l'horloge du grand marionnettiste» [the great puppeteer's clock] the work of Monestier, Institut International des Arts de la Marionnette.
Left, bust of Arthur Rimbaud. Opposite page, the monumental mill (17th century).
Pages 70-71, the loop of the Meuse at Monthermé; the old town, left bank, around the fortified church, St-Sever, (15th century), view from «La Roche à Sept Heure», right bank.

SEDAN. For many years the seigniory was the property of Mouzon abbey, upstream on the Meuse, itself owned by the archbishops of Reims, from the 9th to the 14th century. This place and twenty one villages formed a principality, sold in 1424 to the counts of Marck, dukes of Bouillon. This House maintained a privileged relationship with the House of France, at whose side it was almost always found. Henri Robert de la Marck and Françoise de Bourbon, his wife, supporters of the Reformation, were converted in 1562 and made Sedan «little Geneva», an asylum town, founding a well-known academy and humanist college. There were up to seventeen pastors and public life was subject to strict puritanism. The beautiful neo-classical temple dates from this period, converted into a church after the Revocation of the Edict of Nantes. Through his marriage to Charlotte de la Marck, in 1591, Henri de la Tour d'Auvergne, viscount of Turenne, became prince of Sedan and duke of Bouillon. The La Tour d'Auvergnes were to be involved in all the plotting until the occupation of the Principality by Fabert who administered it on the king's behalf from 1642 to 1662. The cloth industry then expanded rapidly with the construction of a large factory. Some beautiful 17th and 18th century residences, recall the prosperity of Sedan in the classical period. The princes made some improvements to the fortress in the second half of the 16th century creating one of the leading citadels in Europe. The «château-bas», at the foot of the fortress, dating from the early 17th century, offered more convenient living accommodation than that of the fortress. Salomon de Brosse, a relative of the prince, was probably the architect. It was here that Henri de Turenne, the future marshal, was born in 1611.

The name Sedan is still associated with the unhappy memory of Napoleon III's capitulation on 2 September 1870, after the heroic resistance of 100.000 men against 250.000 Prussians.

OUZONVILLE. On the right bank of the Meuse, in the Goubelle valley, which descends from the wooded heights of les Grandes Hazelles, e industrial town, with its forges and foundries, is still near a salubrious natural setting of rocks and woods, beside the busy river.

THE LEGEND OF THE FOUR AYMON SONS. In this long, 13th century, tale of epic adventure - 18.500 alexandrines - the episodes were directly inspired by Charlemagne's iniquitous behaviour, in violation of the principles of chivalry. All are linked, from misfortune to misfortune, in the Classical manner, as if destiny, by perverting the suzerain's sense of honour, must end in tragedy: Aymon de Dordone supports his brother, duke Beuve d'Aygremont, a rebel vassal of Charles. Peace is made. Aymon takes his four sons, Aalard, Renaud, Guichard and Richard to the Emperor's court where Charles arms them as knights. Alas! Renaud quarrels with Bertolai, Charles' nephew, over a game of chess. Bertolai strikes and wounds Renaud. Renaud complains to Charles, but receives, not recompense from him, but another blow. Renaud, wounded in flesh and honour, kills Bertolai. He flees with his three brothers into the forest of Ardenne, on Bayard, Renaud's enchanted horse, which carries all four without tiring. For seven years they live in the château of Montessor that they built, unbeknownst to the Emperor. When Charles learns of it, he besieges the château; and through treason, takes it. The four sons flee on Bayard and live as outlaws deep in the forest, on game, roots and fruit, drinking water from the rushing streams. Thin and dirty, in rags, they go to the château of Dordone, although their father Aymon, on oath to the Emperor, is compelled to reject and pursue them. Fortunately, their mother recognises them, gives them food and drink and provides them with the equipment they need. They resume their wanderings, accompanied by their good cousin, Maugis the enchanter.

The next tale takes them into Gascony where the brothers are received by King Yon, whose sister, Aelis, marries Renaud. They build the powerful château of Montauban. Charles leads his army into Gascony to capture the brothers and Maugis. His knights show reluctance. Betrayed by Yon,

Renaud and his brothers just manage to escape an ambush, saved by Maugis. After numerous episodes: the capture of the wounded Richard, the siege and taking of Montauban, the brothers' withdrawal into their château de Trémoigne, the peace is concluded, on condition that Renaud depart on a pilgrimage to the Holy Sepulchre and hand over Bayard.

The story does not end there, more adventures await Renaud and his sons... Renaud, returned from Jerusalem, distributed his assets, and became a casual labourer on the site of Cologne cathedral. His strength and work, for which he earned a single denier, led to his being killed by the other labourers.

His body, thrown into the Rhine, rose to the surface again, borne by all the fish of the river, it glowed with light and angels sang. Renaud had become

Above, rock and statue of the four Aymon sons. Opposite and Left, Château-Regnault, (Renaud's château) - Page 76, les dames de Meuse, legendary peaks (alt. 402 m. 250 m above river level).

St Renaud. As for Bayard, Charlemagne, wished to avenge himself on him. He had him taken to the bridge over the Meuse at Liège, a millsto hung around his neck and pushed into the river... «If you can't drink it all, you must perish». Bayard was swallowed up by the icy current. The pe were dismayed by such cruelty. But further downstream, the Meuse widens and the horse swam and broke the millstone with his shoe. He cross the river, climbed to the bank, neighed and shook himself dry, stamped his feet and plunged deep into the wild forest of Ardenne. It is said that lives there still. Years ago, when there were horses on farms in Ardenne and Lorraine, they were still sometimes given the name Bayard.

Monthermé (from Mont Ermel from the name of a 6th century bishop), the old town, right bank, the new town, left bank.

REVIN. This land of iron mines and iron casting, later specialising in the manufacture of furnaces, machines and tools, is mentioned in an century charter. The city, run in the late 13th century by the count of Hainaut, later acquired de facto independence, like other walled towns Ardenne, and became French in 1769. The fairly regular layout of the old town resembles that of 13th century new towns. Notre Dame chu was rebuilt in 1706. On the quay to the north some fine 16th century half-timbered houses still stand.

FUMAY. «If the good people of Fumay had as many acres as they have covered roofs with the beautiful purple slate from their quarries, their town would be the largest in the kingdom.» From the end of the 12th century to late in our own, the town was at the centre of the slate trade in the river basin, where long, low walls of slate lined the quays awaiting the boats. Exploitation of the slate quarries ceased in the early 1970's; but metallurgy remains. On the quay of the Meuse, two houses bear a 17th century date and the old town rises in terraces on the isthmus that forms the bend in the river.

Previous page: Tall purple foxgloves, biennial and toxic, with flowers shaped like the fingers of a glove, like the clearings, edges and gaps of forests growing in acid and siliceous soils.

HAYBES. Fumay's neighbour shared with it the exploitation of the slate quarries. For lovers of unspoiled nature it is the perfect place to stay, amid vast forested areas on the heights either side the Meuse, Haybes wood, Catoir wood, Fépin wood and many others. It is a peaceful and delightful staging post on one of the oldest routes in Europe, the Meuse; today pleasure boats mingle with the barges laden with goods that they carry the full length of the river between the Netherlands and France.

VIREUX-MOLHAIN. The founders of Molhain believed in the virtues of running water and settled between the rivers. The Luve stream rus[...] down from Franche-Forêt, between the woods of Mazée and the Hospice at Harscamps, to join the winding course of the Viroin, just befor[...] combines with the Meuse. A Gallo-Roman fort on Mont Vireux *(below right)* guarded the southern approach on the left bank of the river and was u[...] until the 14th century. St-Martin de Molhain church, of Carolingian origin, was reconstructed in the 18th century and decorated in the Italian style.

SLATE AND SLATE QUARRIES. The slate deposits of Ardennes, exploited initially on the surface, then along underground seams, supplied dark and light purple slate at Fumay and Haybes, and grey-blue or green at Rimognes. From the 12th century they were used to roof the abbeys, churches and châteaux of Picardy, the Ile de France and Champagne, then, belatedly, replaced thatch after urban fires. Exploitation ceased in the late 20th century.

IVET. Where the Meuse and the roads crossing the Ardennes hills meet, a Roman garrison held the left bank where Givet-St-Hilaire was to be uilt. On the Right bank, at Givet-Notre-Dame, the bishop of Maastricht, Saint-Hubert, owned a demesne in the 8th century. From the 11th century ivet-St-Hilaire belonged to the Chiny family. At the end of the 11th century a fortified bridge, demolished in the 14th century, connected the two anks. After the attack by François 1, in 1554, Charles-Quint constructed the fortress of Charlemont. On the right bank, Henri II modernised the efences of Mont d'Haurs, whose tower dominates the Meuse. After the treaty of Nimègue (1679), Louis XIV charged Vauban with adapting the aces and citadels on both banks to the new strategies, he had a pontoon bridge installed, replaced in 1804 by a stone bridge, and had Givet-St-ilaire rebuilt in brick and Givet blue stone. The church, built by an engineer, is crowned with a complex object which amused Victor Hugo. Givet--Hilaire, birthplace of Méhul, the composer (1763), has retained its 17th century character *(below and page 84)*. Givet Notre-Dame *(above)* has ted for the textile industry, metallurgy and a port.

ROCROI. On a plateau, facing the Spanish fortified towns, Henri II fortified this marshy and open site. The Spanish twice tried to take it. The Calvinists of Sedan, who had taken it, ceded it to the Guise family. Louis XIII purchased it in 1614, and reinforced it. By 19 May 1643 the Spanish army and its incomparable infantry were at the gates of Rocroi. Louis II de Bourbon, duke of Enghien and future Prince de Condé, and 21 years old, arrived from Péronne with the royal army. His boldness and manoeuvres crushed the enemy in seven hours. Ten years later the same Condé, a frondeur, took the town for the Spanish. Louis XIV was to complete the place through Vauban and it was to remain operational until 1883.

LA SEMOIS. Its source is at Arlon, in Belgian Luxembourg and it winds through the land, threading its way around so many rocky and woode promontories, that it covers, with loops and detours, two hundred kilometres, although only seventy-five kilometres from the Meuse as the crow flies. enters France upstream of Haute-Rivières *(above)* which borders the right bank in one long street. Once over the border, capriciously, it is spelle Semoy. Downstream, the villages of Nohan and Naux, dominated by the ruins of the ephemeral château of Linchamps above them, built and destroye in the 16th century; it then descends to the boroughs of Thilay *(below)*, then Navaux, Haulmé and Tournavaux, before the confluence at Monthermé.

HIERGES. From the keep, from early feudal times, the lord had a watch kept for the merchants on the road between Germany and France, and on the Meuse, to collect his tolls. A powerful château was built by successive lords. In the 16th century, the fort belonged to the Berlaymont, general officers to Charles-Quint and was assailed by the French then rebuilt, but unfortunately was set on fire in 1793.

RENWEZ. The forest museum presents reminders of the traditional crafts of the great Ardennes forest, some 150 000 hectares. Figures of woodcutters, carpenters, pit sawyers, charcoal burners, clog-makers made from oak logs hinged together, show the tools, gestures and habitat of people apart, hidden under the cover of the oaks. These artisans and men of nature would soon be forgotten without this model educational exhibition of forest traditions.

LES VIEILLES FORGES. To the north of the Bois de Renwez, a lake is created by the dam where the course of the many springs of the plateau ends. In summer, bathers slip into its cool waters or bask on the sand, their eyes following the subtle interplay of sails and wind against the background of the forests. In winter, the woods are the colour of wild boar and the waters reflect the skudding clouds in the sky above.

GRANDPRE. This county seat of one of Champagne's counties, defended the pass north of Argonne, where the river Aire runs. It suffered enormously during the Hundred Years War, from cavalry expeditions and the confiscation of several fiefs by the counts of Bar. When France was once more in the hands of Louis XI, he gave the place to the house of Joyeuse, famous in Ardèche and loyal to the crown of France, to secure this strategic route in the north of the kingdom. The Joyeuse family retained it until the 18th century. The great 16th century château was burned to the ground in 1834. There remains, between two outbuildings, the brick and stone portal constructed in 1598 on the orders of Claude de Joyeuse. The three gates are protected by three gatehouses topped with elegant broken pediments while two twisted columns, in the baroque style, frame the great portal. The 13th to 16th century St-Médard church, considerably altered, has the same proportions as the old château. The tombs of Claude de Joyeuse († 1629) and his wife, the countess, can be seen here.

VOUZIERS. Honoured by François I, during the war waged in the region against Charles Quint, in 1516 the village was granted the privile by the king of an annual fair, and became a town. It needed a church appropriate to its new status. Thus in 1517 began to rise before the Maurille entrance, which dated from the 15th century, the three porches of a monumental Renaissance façade. This first floor seems to have be finished in 1548, or in 1565, according to other indications. The two upper levels, that architectural logic suggests would have been qu magnificent, were never built because of the Wars of Religion. In the reveals of the portals scalloped niches form porticoes where statues were stand. The same niches are found between the portals, with a pediment, surmounted by other niches where the evangelists stand beneath hi canopies. The central tympanum portrays the Annunciation, a skeleton on the left tympanum, portrays Judgement or death, while that on the rig shows Christ arisen. In 1769 with the final abandonment of the project, this unfinished façade was connected to the nave by two bays, covering as if it were a hall, with a slate roof and a large structure of the same material, as a clock tower.

Opposite page, l'hôtel-de-ville [town hall] (1924) and the central tympanum of St-Mauri

RETHEL. From its hill, the county town commanded the passage across the Aisne. A keep stood on the fortified motte. At the foot of the ca was the Town enclosed by walls. Taken and retaken in the course of every war, it was almost entirely destroyed by the Germans in June 1940, wl defended by General de Lattre de Tassigny. The church, refurbished between 1512 and 1531 in the flamboyant style, is double: on the left hand s are the Notre Dame side aisle and nave, for the Benedictines (until 1740), and on the right the St-Nicolas nave and side aisle for the parish.

CONTENTS

Photographies of ESTEL Editions
With the collaboration of MM.
P- Viard, Dino Sassi.
D. Chagot (Boars P. 75)
P. Mertès (P. 95)
Translations: ILS Paris Service de Langues
Printed in the E.C.C. - Legal deposit: 2 nd quarter 2001
I.S.B.N. 2-912426-02-2